Excel 2019 Advanced Topics

Leverage More Powerful Tools to Enhance Your Productivity

NATHAN GEORGE

CONTENTS

INTRODUCTION

Excel 2019 Advanced Topics covers a selection of topics that will enable you to take advantage of more powerful features in Excel 2019 in creating quick and robust solutions for your data. My *Excel 2019 Basics* book covered the essentials of Excel and how to use Excel tools to create solutions for common Excel tasks. *Excel 2019 Advanced Topics* does not rehash the content of that book. Rather, it goes beyond the basics and covers intermediate to advanced topics. This book aims to provide you with tools and techniques that enable you to solve data challenges that require more than just a basic knowledge of Excel.

With *Excel 2019 Advanced Topics,* you'll learn how to use features that make Excel one of the best data processing and analysis tools in the market. The topics covered include, automating Excel tasks with macros, analyzing alternate data sets and creating data projections with What-If Analysis, analyzing large data sets with pivot tables and pivot charts, solving complex problems with advanced functions, consolidating data from different worksheets, removing duplicate data, troubleshooting formula errors, and many more. Unlike many other books, this book does not only show you how to use specific features but also in what context those features need to be used.

Who Is This Book For?

Excel 2019 Advanced Topics is for you if you want to go beyond the basics and become an Excel power user. In this book, you'll learn how to use some of the more powerful tools to address complex tasks and create quicker results. This is not an exhaustive guide on advanced Excel, but a selection of intermediate to advanced topics relevant to real-world productivity tasks you're likely to encounter at home or work requiring more than a basic knowledge of Excel.

This book assumes you have some basic knowledge of Excel. For brevity, *Excel 2019 Advanced Topics* does not cover the topics already covered in my *Excel 2019 Basics* book (unless necessary for the flow of the lesson). If you need to brush up on the basics (or if you're new to Excel), then my *Excel 2019 Basics* book covers all the fundamentals you'll need.

Excel 2019 Advanced Topics is aimed at readers with Microsoft Excel 2019, but many of the core Excel features remain the same for earlier versions of the software like Excel 2016 and 2013. So, you will still find many of the lessons in this book relevant if you have an earlier version of Excel.

As much as possible, I point out the features new in Excel 2019 when covered. Note however that if you're using an earlier version of Excel, some of the file-related tasks described in this book may not match your old version of Excel. This is due to Microsoft changing command options and dialog boxes for many file-related tasks compared to older versions.

How to Use This Book

This book can be used as a step-by-step training guide as well as a reference manual that you come back to from time to time. You can read it cover to cover or skip to certain parts that cover topics you want to learn. Although the chapters have been organised logically, the book has been designed to enable you to read a chapter as a standalone tutorial to learn how to carry out a certain task.

There are many ways to carry out the same task in Excel, so, for brevity, I have focused on the most efficient way of carrying out a task. On some occasions, however, I also provided alternative ways to carry out a task.

As much as possible, the menu items and commands mentioned are bolded to distinguish them from the other text. I have also included many images to illustrate the features and tasks being discussed.

Assumptions

The software and hardware assumptions made when writing this book is that you already have Excel 2019 installed on your computer and that you're working on the Windows 10 platform.

Important: Excel 2019 is the first version of Excel that is not compatible with previous versions of Windows. If you have an earlier version of Windows, for example, Windows 7 or 8, and you're subscribed to Microsoft 365, then the newest version of Excel you can run will be Excel 2016. Excel 2016 has all the power of Excel 2019 apart from a few added features and some screens that look different. If you are running Excel 2016 you can still use this book (as long as you're aware that some of the screens shown may look slightly different).

If you are using Excel 2019 on a Mac, then simply substitute any Windows keyboard commands mentioned in the book for the Mac equivalent. All the features within Excel remain the same for both platforms.

If you're using Excel on a tablet or touchscreen device, again, simply substitute any keyboard commands mentioned in the book with the equivalent on your touchscreen device.

Practice Files

Downloadable Excel files have been provided to save you a lot of typing if you want to practice in Excel as you follow the examples in the book. All examples are fully detailed in the book and these files have simply been provided to save you some typing, so they're optional. You can practice by changing the data to view different results. Please note that practice files have only been included for chapters where the examples use a sizable amount of sample data. You can download the files from the following link:

https://www.excelbytes.com/atdownload

Notes:
- Ensure you type in all characters in the URL in your browser's address bar. If you encounter an error, double-check that you have typed in the URL correctly.

- The files have been zipped into one download. Windows 10 comes with the functionality to unzip files. If your OS does not have this functionality, you'll need to get a piece of software like WinZip or WinRAR to unzip the file. You'll need to have Excel installed on your computer to open and use these files (preferably Excel 2013 and above).

- If you are having any problems downloading the file, please contact me at **support@excelbytes.com**. Include the title of this book in your email and the practice files will be emailed directly to you.

Improvements in Excel 2019

Ink Improvements

Improved inking and drawing features are available under Draw that enables you to use a drawing tablet to enter math formulas or freestyle drawing in your worksheet.

Better Cell Selection

Have your ever selected too many cells on your worksheet or the wrong ones? You can now deselect cells you don't want to be part of your selection without having to start over.

Improved Autocomplete

The autocomplete is 'smarter' in Excel 2019. For example, let's say you want to use the FORMULATEXT function, but you can't remember the exact spelling, you can just type in =TEXT and the autocomplete menu will list all the functions that contain "TEXT" in their name, including FORMULATEXT. In previous editions, you would need to start spelling the name correctly for autocomplete to find it.

Office Themes

You can now apply four Office Themes to Excel: Colorful (default), Dark Gray, Black, and White. To change your Excel theme, go to **File > Account** and then select a theme from the **Office Theme** drop-down list. Note that the theme you choose will be applied across all your Microsoft 365 applications.

Translate Words to Other Languages

You can now translate a word or phrase to another language with Microsoft Translator. You can access this feature from the **Translate** button on the **Review** tab in the ribbon.

1. WORKING WITH MULTIPLE WORKBOOKS

There are occasions when you need to work with several open workbooks and Excel 2019 provides several features that make it easier to work with multiple windows.

In this chapter, we will cover how to:

- Switch between multiple open workbooks.
- View multiple workbooks side-by-side.
- Arrange all open workbooks on your screen.
- Split the screen of your worksheet.
- Move data between workbooks.
- Move worksheets between workbooks.

1.1 Managing Multiple Windows

To work with multiple workbooks, open the main one and then open all the others.

Switch Between Workbooks

To switch between workbooks, on the **View** tab, in the **Window** group, click **Switch Windows**. Select the workbook you want to switch to from the dropdown menu.

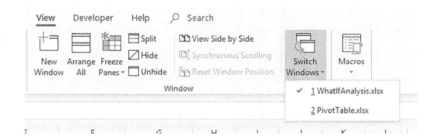

View Side-By-Side

To view worksheets from the different workbooks you've opened at the same time, you can manually arrange them on your screen or use an excel command to automatically tile them.

On the **View** tab, in the **Windows** group, click on the **View Side by Side** button. Toggle the **Side by Side** button to switch between a full screen of the active workbook and two workbooks.

If you have only two workbooks open, Excel will place the last one you opened above the earlier one. If you have more than two workbooks open, Excel will display the **Compare Side by Side** dialog box to allow you to select the workbook that you want to place side by side with the active one.

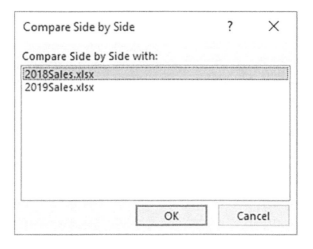

Arrange All

If you need to compare more than two workbooks on the same screen:

1. On the **View** tab, click the **Arrange All** button.

   The **Arrange Windows** dialog box will be displayed giving you the Arrange options of **Tiled**, **Horizontal**, **Vertical**, and **Cascading**.

2. Select one of the options, making sure you leave the **Windows of Active Workbook** unchecked and click **OK**.

New Window

To create a new window of the same document so that you can work in different places at the same time

On the **View** tab, in the **Window** group, click on the **New Window** button. This will open a new window of the same workbook (note that this does not create a new file).

To view the windows of the same workbook side-by-side:

1. On the **View** tab, in the Window group, click on the **Arrange All** button.

2. Select an Arrange option, for example, Vertical.

3. Click the **Windows of active workbook** checkbox to select it.

4. Click **OK** to complete the action and close the Arrange Windows dialog box.

The windows of the same workbook will now the arranged side by side.

Split Screen

The split screen method allows you to split your worksheet so that you can see different parts of the worksheet in the same window. This comes in handy when you have a large amount of data and you would like to see different parts of the screen while working on the data.

To split the screen of a worksheet, do the following:

1. On the **View** tab, in the **Window** group, click on the **Split** button.

    A horizontal and vertical dividing line will split the screen into four parts with a scroll bar for each part. You can adjust the position of these dividers with your mouse pointer depending on how you want the layout.

2. To move a dividing line, for example, the horizontal one, place your mouse pointer over the divider and it will change to a double-headed

arrow. You can now move the divider up or down, depending on how you want to view the split screen. You can do the same for the vertical line.

1.2 Moving Data Between Workbooks

There are two ways you can copy or move data between open workbooks.

Method 1

First, arrange the workbooks so that the worksheets you want to work with are visible side-by-side on the screen.

Select the range of cells in the source worksheet, then on the **Home** tab, click the **Copy** button (or press the **Ctrl+C** keys) to copy the data, or click the **Cut** button (or press the **Ctrl+X** keys) to move the data.

At the destination worksheet, select the top leftmost cell of the area where you want to paste the data and on the **Home** tab, click **Paste** (or press the **Ctrl+V** keys) to paste the data.

Method 2

The second method you can use to move or copy data between screens is to drag and drop the data from one workbook to the other.

Use the following steps to drag and drop data:

1. Select the data in the source worksheet.

2. Move the mouse pointer over the edge of the selected range until it turns into a crosshair (see image below).

16

$10,227	$8,343	$5,467	$9,002
$13,263	$10,201	$6,199	$12,083
$13,680	$9,565	$14,089	$6,906
$5,610	$6,557	$5,756	$9,387
$11,335	$6,363	$5,980	$12,584
$10,214	$5,270	$11,708	$7,479
$5,746	$8,398	$6,390	$8,263
$5,594	$11,446	$7,794	$5,736
$14,537	$11,826	$8,848	$9,674
$9,118	$5,774	$7,533	$11,096
$13,417	$12,864	$13,032	$10,514
$6,573	$8,805	$13,254	$9,397

3. Once the pointer has changed to a crosshair, click and drag the selection to the other worksheet window.

4. At the destination worksheet window, you'll see a rectangle representing the area containing the data to be pasted. Drag it to the left topmost cell of the range where you want to place the data and release the mouse button.

   Note: To copy the data instead of moving it, hold down the **Ctrl** key as you drag the data across to the other window.

5. After you release the mouse button, you may get a prompt that says: *"There's a problem with the clipboard, but you can still paste your content within this workbook."* Just click **OK** to dismiss the prompt and complete the action.

1.3 Moving Worksheets Between Workbooks

Method 1: Using Move or Copy

1. Open both the source workbook that contains worksheets to be moved or copied and the destination workbook where the worksheets will be placed. You need to open both the source and destination to copy or move worksheets between them.

2. On the **View** tab, use the **Arrange All** command to arrange the windows side-by-side, preferably using the **Vertical** option.

3. Click on the workbook with the worksheets that need to be moved or copied to activate it. Next, click on the sheet tab at the bottom of the screen to select it (to select more than one worksheet, hold down the **Ctrl** key as you click on the individual sheet tabs).

4. On the **Home** tab, click on the **Format** button and select **Move or Copy Sheet...** from the menu. This displays the **Move or Copy** dialog box.

5. In the Move or Copy dialog box, select the destination workbook in the **To Book** field. In the **Before sheet** field select where you want to place the worksheet inside the destination workbook.

    To create a copy of the worksheet, rather than move it, select the **Create a copy** checkbox.

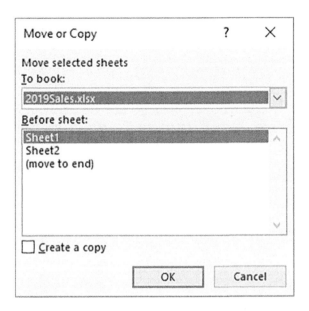

6. Click **OK** to complete the move or copy action and close the dialog box.

Method 2: Using Drag and Drop

Just as you can copy data in a range between workbooks using drag-and-drop, you can also move or copy worksheets between workbooks using drag-and-drop.

To move or copy worksheets between workbooks using drag-and-drop do the following:

1. Arrange the workbooks side-by-side so that you can see both on the screen. You can do this manually or use the **Arrange All** command described above. Preferably you should arrange them vertically.

2. Click on the sheet tab in the destination workbook to select the worksheet to be moved or copied (to select more than one, hold down the **Ctrl** key as you click on the individual sheet tabs).

3. Drag the sheet from the source workbook across to the destination workbook with your mouse. You'll see a little document icon representing the sheet you're moving.

Note: To copy the sheet (instead of moving it), hold down the **Ctrl** key as you drag the sheet from the source workbook to the destination workbook. The document icon will have a plus sign (+) if you're copying the sheet.

4. At the destination workbook, you'll see a small arrow, indicating where the sheet would be placed. You can move this arrow left and right to choose where you want to place the sheet before releasing the mouse button to place the sheet there.

This is a much faster way to move or copy worksheets between two open workbooks.

2. TRANSFORM DATA WITH DATA TOOLS

I n this chapter, we will cover how to use some of the data tools provided in Excel 2019 to quickly perform data organizing tasks.

In this chapter we will cover how to:

- Find and remove duplicate rows in your data.
- Find and delete blank rows in your data.
- Convert text to columns.
- Consolidate data from different worksheets into one worksheet.

2.1 Remove Duplicates

On some occasions, you may have a data set, for example, a list of customers you want to use for a mail merge. You want to make sure that you don't have duplicate records before you start the mail merge process so that you don't send the mail to the same customer more than once.

To remove duplicates in Excel, do the following:

1. Click in any cell in the range.

2. On the **Data** tab, in the **Data Tools** group, click on the **Remove Duplicates** button. The **Remove Duplicates** dialog box will be displayed.

3. Leave all the columns selected (if you want the full row checked against one another) and click on **OK**.

4. A message will be displayed telling you if any duplicates were found and how many records were deleted. Click **OK** to complete the process.

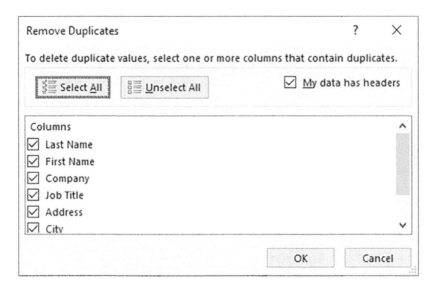

Note: You may have cases where you only want to use a few columns to check for duplicate records. For example, you may have more than one person on your list from the same address, but you only want each address once for the mail merge. In that case, in the Remove Duplicates dialog box, you should deselect all the other columns and only leave the columns you want to use to check for duplicates selected.

Tip: You can also use the Power Query Editor to remove duplicate rows. See the section **Delete Blank Rows** below for how to open and use the Power Query Editor to transform your data.

2.2 Delete Blank Rows

There may be occasions when you have unnecessary blank rows in your data that you want to remove. If you have a large list with a lot of empty rows, it could be time-consuming to manually find and delete the empty rows. Thankfully, there are ways you can do this automatically. We will cover two methods for achieving this task here. The first will be using commands on the Excel Ribbon and the second method involves using the Power Query Editor, which has a command for deleting blank rows.

Method 1

There is no direct command for deleting blank rows on the Ribbon, but you can combine a couple of commands to achieve the task.

To delete blank rows, do the following:
1. Click on the **Home** tab, and then the **Find & Select** button in the Editing group.
2. Select **Go To Special** from the dropdown menu.
3. On the Go To Special screen select **Blanks** and click **OK**.

Excel will select the blank cells in the range.

	A	B	C	D	E
1		New York	Los Angeles	London	Paris
2	Jan	$547.00	$934.00	$412.00	$447.00
3	Feb	$880.00	$590.00	$961.00	$605.00
4	Mar	$717.00	$961.00	$460.00	$652.00
5					
6	Apr	$540.00	$542.00	$574.00	$754.00
7	May	$620.00	$497.00	$531.00	$462.00
8	Jun	$423.00	$874.00	$799.00	$699.00
9	Jul	$937.00	$755.00	$877.00	$446.00
10					
11	Aug	$683.00	$715.00	$792.00	$742.00
12	Sep	$633.00	$421.00	$877.00	$576.00
13	Oct	$551.00	$941.00	$675.00	$598.00
14	Nov	$680.00	$520.00	$867.00	$916.00
15	Dec	$766.00	$524.00	$401.00	$707.00

4. On the Home tab, in the Cells group, click **Delete** > **Delete Sheet Rows**.

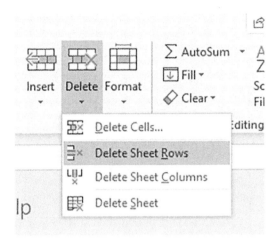

And that's it! This will delete all the rows that were identified and selected using the Go To Special command.

Tip: If you mistakenly deleted rows that you don't want to delete, you can undo your changes by clicking the **Undo** button on the Quick Access Toolbar to reverse your changes.

Method 2

The second method involves using the Power Query Editor in Excel 2019.

To delete blank rows using the Power Query Editor, do the following:

1. Select the data list for which you want to remove blank rows.

    Tip: To quickly select a range, click on the top-left cell of the range, hold down the **Shift** key, and click on the bottom-right cell.

2. On the **Data** tab, in the **Get & Transform Data** group, click the **From Table/Range** command button.

    This will open and display your data in the **Power Query Editor,** which is a supplementary tool in Excel 2019 with a separate user interface and command buttons.

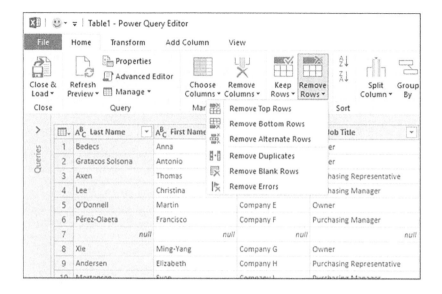

3. On the **Home** tab of the Power Query Editor, click the drop-down arrow on the **Remove Rows** command button, and select **Remove Blank Rows** from the drop-down menu.

   Excel deletes all the blank rows identified in the data list.

4. To save your transformed data, on the **Home** tab of the Power Query Editor, click the **Close & Load** command button to paste the transformed data in a new sheet in your workbook and close the Power Query Editor.

That's it! Your data list without the blank rows will now be in a new sheet with the original data list unchanged. Note that, among other commands, you can also use the Power Query Editor to remove duplicate rows.

2.3 Convert Text to Columns

If you work with a lot of data from different sources, there could be occasions where you receive a text file with values that are separated by commas. When you copy and paste the values in Excel, it would place them all in one column. You can separate these values into different columns using the text to columns command.

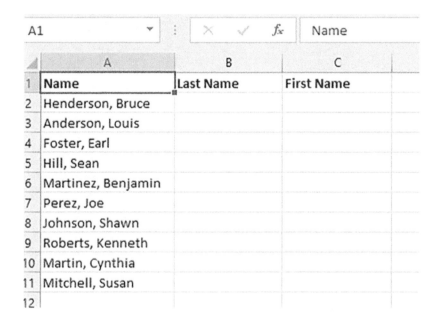

To convert delimited text values into separate columns, do the following:

1. Select the range that contains the text you want to split.

2. On the **Data** tab click on **Text to Columns**.

3. In the Convert Text to Columns Wizard, select **Delimited** and click on **Next**.

4. Select the **Delimiters** for your data. For our example (above), the delimiters are **Comma** and **Space**. You also have the options of Tab, Semicolon, and Other, which allows you to specify the delimiter if it's not one of the default options.

   The **Data preview** portion of the screen shows you a preview of how your data would look after the conversion.

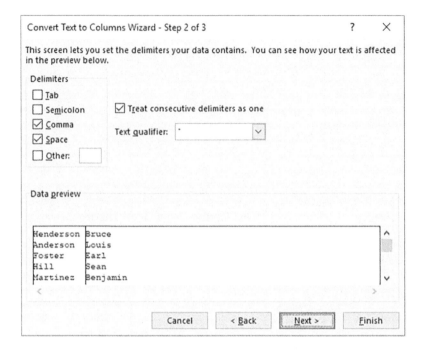

5. Click on **Next**.

6. At the next screen, select the **Column data format** or use what Excel chooses for you.

7. In the **Destination** field, click the up arrow, and on your worksheet, select the top leftmost cell where you want the split data to appear. The cell reference for the destination will be entered in the field.

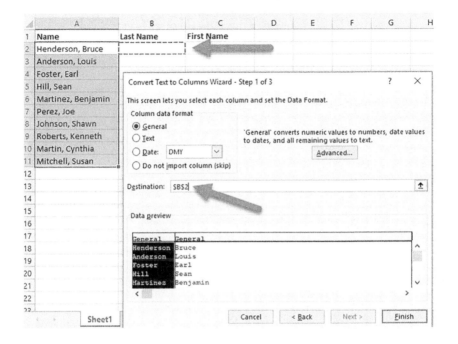

8. Click on **Finish**.

The delimited text will now be split into different columns. You can delete the initial column with the original text from the worksheet or move it to another sheet if you want to keep it.

	A	B	C
1	Name	Last Name	First Name
2	Henderson, Bruce	Henderson	Bruce
3	Anderson, Louis	Anderson	Louis
4	Foster, Earl	Foster	Earl
5	Hill, Sean	Hill	Sean
6	Martinez, Benjamin	Martinez	Benjamin
7	Perez, Joe	Perez	Joe
8	Johnson, Shawn	Johnson	Shawn
9	Roberts, Kenneth	Roberts	Kenneth
10	Martin, Cynthia	Martin	Cynthia
11	Mitchell, Susan	Mitchell	Susan
12			

2.4 Data Consolidation

Data consolidation provides an easy way to combine data from multiple worksheets in a single worksheet. You can consolidate data from different worksheets in the same workbook, different workbooks, or a combination of both. The process allows you to select the ranges you want to add to the consolidation from different sources and Excel will aggregate the data in another workbook.

To consolidate data, all the ranges to be included in the consolidation must be of the same shape and size. For example, let's say we have sales data from 2017 to 2019 that we want to consolidate from three worksheets into one worksheet named **Sales for 2017 – 2019**.

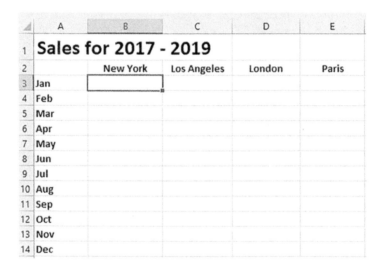

The three workbooks we will be consolidating the data from are:
- 2017Sales.xlsx
- 2018Sales.xlsx
- 2019Sales.xlsx

To consolidate cell ranges from the three workbooks:

1. First, you need to open the destination workbook, that is, the workbook into which you want to consolidate your data. In our example, it will be 2017_2019Sales.xlsx.

2. Open the source workbooks, that is, the workbooks supplying the data you want to consolidate. For our example, the source workbooks are the three workbooks listed above.

3. Switch to the workbook into which you want to consolidate your data. Click on the **Data** tab and click the **Consolidate** button in the **Data Tools** group.

    The Consolidate dialog box will be displayed.

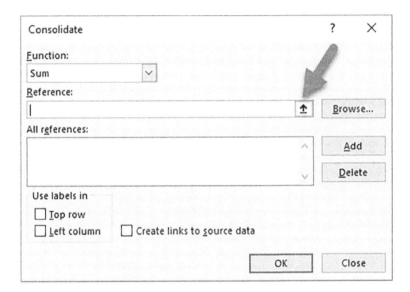

4. On the **Reference** field, click the **Collapse Dialog** button (at the right edge of the field) to collapse the dialog box. When you click this button, it will minimise the Consolidate dialog box.

5. Now you need to select the range from the first worksheet. On the **View** tab, in the **Window** group, click **Switch Windows**. This will display a list of all open workbooks.

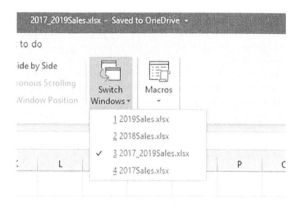

6. Click the first workbook that contains data you want to include in your consolidation. This will make the workbook the active window.

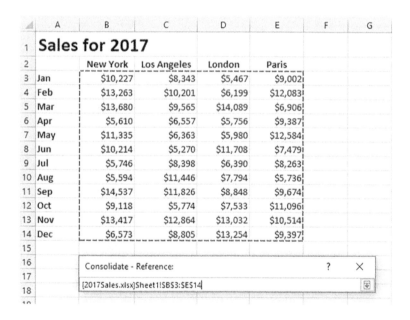

7. Select the cells you want to consolidate, then click the **Expand Dialog** button to return the Consolidate dialog box to its full size.

8. Click **Add** to add the selected range to the **All references** list box.

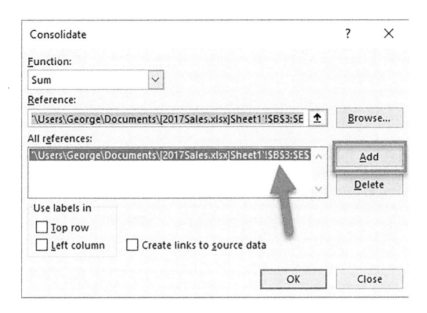

9. Repeat the steps 4 to 8 above to add additional ranges to the consolidation. These ranges can come from different workbooks or different worksheets in the same workbook. For our example, these would be from *2018Sales.xlsx* and *2019Sales.xlsx*.

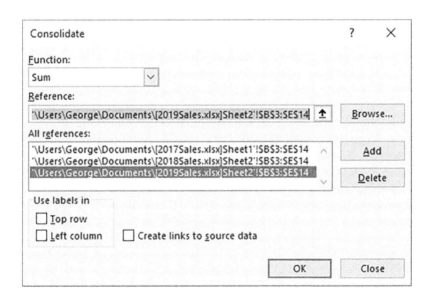

10. The default function used to aggregate the data in the consolidated workbook is **Sum**. You can change this to another function like Count or Average, for example, by clicking the **Function** drop-down list and selecting a different function.

11. Click **OK** when you've added all the ranges to be consolidated.

	A	B	C	D	E
1	**Sales for 2017 - 2019**				
2		New York	Los Angeles	London	Paris
3	Jan	$29,515	$27,631	$29,693	$19,726
4	Feb	$33,126	$30,064	$18,811	$26,229
5	Mar	$38,592	$34,477	$41,211	$30,876
6	Apr	$18,162	$22,023	$18,734	$22,527
7	May	$31,523	$29,097	$20,000	$25,832
8	Jun	$35,671	$23,079	$24,754	$36,707
9	Jul	$28,859	$34,226	$26,289	$27,339
10	Aug	$18,148	$39,842	$29,510	$29,486
11	Sep	$26,687	$32,604	$24,378	$33,720
12	Oct	$38,590	$19,248	$26,325	$29,174
13	Nov	$23,903	$30,672	$35,400	$38,724
14	Dec	$20,449	$33,015	$24,878	$24,997

Each cell in the consolidated data will now hold the sum for that cell from all the other worksheets.

3. USING EXTERNAL DATA

W hen working with Excel, you often have situations when you have to import data from other applications into Excel. The most common are comma-separated files (CSV) or some other form of delimitation.

In this chapter, we will cover how to import data from:
- A Microsoft Access database.
- A delimited text file, for example, a CSV file.
- A website with constantly changing live data, for example, Forex data.

3.1 Importing Data from Microsoft Access

To import data from an Access Database, do the following:

1. Click on the **Data** tab, in the **Get & Transform Data** group, click **Get Data**, then select **From Database** > **From Microsoft Access Database**.

2. At the **Import Data** dialog box, navigate to the Access database (this will usually be an *.accdb or *.mdb file) and then click the **Import** button.

The **Navigator** dialog box is displayed. This dialog box is divided into two panes: On the left, there is a list of tables and queries and on the right, there is a preview. When you click an item on the left pane, a preview is displayed on the right showing the fields in the table.

To import more than one table from the selected Access database, click the **Select Multiple Items** checkbox on the left pane. Excel will then display check boxes against each item on the list, which allows you to select more than one table from the list.

3. After you've selected the table(s) you want to import, click on the **Load** button to import the data. It will be imported into a new worksheet as an Excel table with all the Table tools available.

ID	Product Code	Product Name	Description	Standard Cost	List Price	Reorder Level
1	NWTB-1	Northwind Traders Chai		13.5	18	
3	NWTCO-3	Northwind Traders Syrup		7.5	10	
4	NWTCO-4	Northwind Traders Cajun Seasoning		16.5	22	
5	NWTO-5	Northwind Traders Olive Oil		16.0125	21.35	
6	NWTJP-6	Northwind Traders Boysenberry Spread		18.75	25	
7	NWTDFN-7	Northwind Traders Dried Pears		22.5	30	
8	NWTS-8	Northwind Traders Curry Sauce		30	40	
14	NWTDFN-14	Northwind Traders Walnuts		17.4375	23.25	
17	NWTCFV-17	Northwind Traders Fruit Cocktail		29.25	39	
19	NWTBGM-19	Northwind Traders Chocolate Biscuits Mix		6.9	9.2	
20	NWTJP-6	Northwind Traders Marmalade		60.75	81	
21	NWTBGM-21	Northwind Traders Scones		7.5	10	
34	NWTB-34	Northwind Traders Beer		10.5	14	
40	NWTCM-40	Northwind Traders Crab Meat		13.8	18.4	
41	NWTSO-41	Northwind Traders Clam Chowder		7.2375	9.65	
43	NWTB-43	Northwind Traders Coffee		34.5	46	
48	NWTCA-48	Northwind Traders Chocolate		9.5625	12.75	
51	NWTDFN-51	Northwind Traders Dried Apples		39.75	53	
52	NWTG-52	Northwind Traders Long Grain Rice		5.25	7	
56	NWTP-56	Northwind Traders Gnocchi		28.5	38	

Sheet1 | Access Data

The Navigator dialog box also provides other options for uploading the Access data:

Transform Data

At the bottom of the Navigator dialog box, there is a **Transform Data** button. When you click this button, it will open the **Excel Power Query Editor**, which provides several tools that enable you to transform the data before you import it. For example, you may choose to import only some columns or use a query to select only some of the data.

Load To

For more load options, at the bottom of the Navigator screen, click the **Load** button's drop-down menu, then click the **Load To** menu item to open the **Import Data** dialog box.

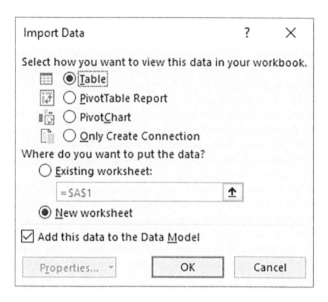

This box allows you to import the Access data as:

- An Excel Table (default)
- A PivotTable
- A PivotChart
- Only a connection to the database.

You can also choose to import the data into an existing worksheet or a new worksheet (default).

3.2 Importing Text files

As Excel stores data in cells, the text files you can import need to have a way of separating the content into different cells. The character that marks this separation is called a *delimiter* because it marks the "limit" of a value.

The most common delimiter used for text files is the comma. For example, you may have the sequence 200, 400, 100, 900 to represent data in four cells. The text files that use a comma as a delimiter are called comma-separated values (CSV) files.

There are occasions when text files need to use different delimiters when a comma might not be an appropriate delimiter. For example, using a comma delimiter may present a problem for financial figures (like $100,000) because commas are part of the values. Hence some financial data programs export their data by using the tab character as a delimiter and these files are referred to as Tab-delimited files.

Follow the steps below to import a text data file into Excel:

1. Click on the **Data** tab, in the **Get & Transform Data** group, select **From File**, then click **From Text/CSV**. This displays the Navigator screen.

    The Navigator examines the data in the text or CSV file and attempts to correctly split it up into separate columns for the worksheet based on the delimiter it identifies as the separator, for example, a comma or a tab.

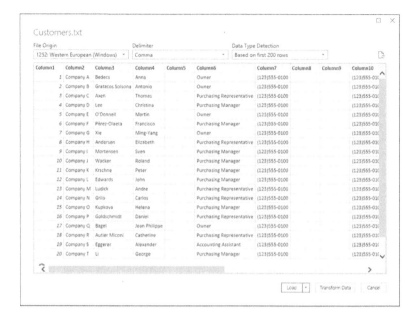

2. As depicted in the image above, on top of the Navigator screen you have three fields. For anything other than complex data requiring advanced knowledge, you should leave **File Origin** and **Data Type Detection** at their default values. The **Delimiter** drop-down list identifies the delimiter used in the text file. If this has been wrongly identified, for example, if your file is a Tab delimited file then you can select a different delimiter from the drop-down list.

3. If Excel correctly parsed the data in your text file as shown in the Navigator's preview, you can then select one of the following options to import the data into your worksheet.

   At the bottom of the screen, you have three options for uploading the data:

   • The **Load** button imports the data as seen in the Navigator preview into your workbook (in a new worksheet).

   • The **Load To** option (on the Load button's drop-down menu) gives you more options for how you want to import the data and where to place the data. The Load To dialog box is discussed above under importing data from Microsoft Access.

- The **Transform Data** button opens the data in the **Excel Power Query Editor**. This enables you to query and transform the data before importing it. For example, you may want to import only a few of the columns in the data set or data that meet some criteria. Transform data allows you to remove the columns you don't want to import.

Tip: If you only want a subset of the data, instead of using **Transform Data**, you can also import the full data into Excel and delete the columns you don't want within Excel.

Using the Convert Text to Columns Wizard

Occasionally, Excel may be unable to correctly parse the data into separate columns even after you change the Delimiter, File Origin, and Data Type Detection. If Excel still insists on importing each row as a single column, you can still import the data and use the **Text to Columns** tool in Excel to split the values into separate columns.

After importing the data into Excel, follow the steps below to split the data into separate columns:

1. In your worksheet, select the cells with the imported data.

2. On the **Data** tab, in the **Data Tools** group, click on the **Text to Columns** button.

   This will open the **Convert Text to Columns Wizard - Step 1 of 3** dialog box.

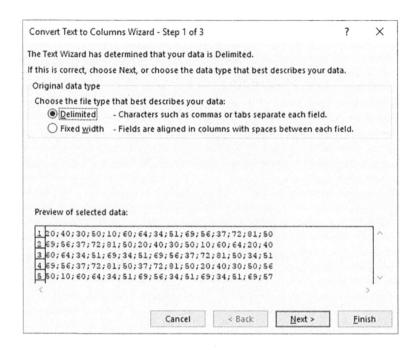

3. On step 1 of the wizard, choose between the **Delimited** and **Fixed width** option, depending on how your data is separated, then click the **Next** button to go to step 2.

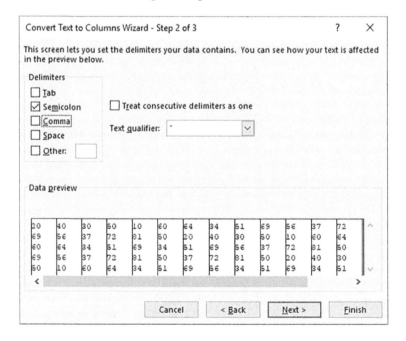

4. If you selected the Delimited option in Step 1 of the wizard, then In Step 2, under the **Delimiters** section, select the delimiting character for your text file. In the example above, the delimiter for our data is a semicolon.

5. If the delimiting character used in your text file is not any of the offered options under Delimiters, then select **Other** and enter the character in its text box. If your file uses more than one delimiting character, for example, a comma and a space, you need to select all their checkboxes including the **Treat Consecutive Delimiters As One** checkbox.

6. By default, the Convert Text to Columns Wizard treats characters enclosed in double-quotes as text entries and not numbers. If your text file uses single quotes, then you would select it from the **Text Qualifier** drop-down list.

   Fixed width files: If your file is a fixed-width separated file and you selected the Fixed width option in step 1 of the wizard, then in step 2, you'll see a preview that allows you to determine the column breaks by clicking in the text area to create column lines. You can drag and resize these column lines to match the column breaks in the text.

7. When you're happy with the preview of the text in step 2, click the **Next** button to go to step 3 of the wizard.

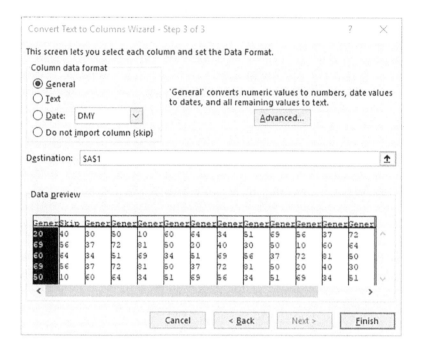

8. In step 3 of the process, you can click on each column in the preview area and select different settings for importing the data under **Column data format**. You can choose between the **General** (default), **Text**, and **Date** data formats, or skip importing the column altogether by selecting **Do not import column (skip)**.

    Tip: You can always import the data using the **General** data format and change the data format within Excel for the columns you want to change.

9. The **Destination** field shows you the top-leftmost cell of the range where the text will be placed. If you want it in a different part of the worksheet then select a different destination by clicking on the up-arrow on the right of the field.

10. Once you're done, click on **Finish** to convert the data.

Excel splits the entries in the imported text file into separate columns in place of the previous data. You can now set the data format (if you didn't do that during the conversion) and adjust the column widths.

Tip: You can directly open some CSV files in Excel and convert them to Excel workbooks. If CSV files are associated with Excel on your computer, you can double click on the file to open it in Excel. Alternatively, you can open the file from within Excel even if the CSV extension is not associated with Excel on your PC. Once you have the file open in Excel and the data is displayed properly, you can then save the file as an Excel workbook.

3.3 Importing Data from a Website

To import data from the web, you first need to identify the web address (URL) of the website with the data you want to import. Then you can use the import tools in Excel to import the data directly from the webpage into your worksheet.

Let's say we want to import currency exchange rates from the web into our worksheet.

Below is how the data looks on the website after we've used the filters on the website to narrow down our search and display the data we want. We can now use this URL to import the data tables on the website.

https://www.xe.com/currencytables/?from=USD&date=2019-05-17

Current and Historical Rate Tables

Build current and historic rate tables with your chosen base currency with XE Currency Tables. For commercial purposes, get an automated currency feed through the XE Currency Data API.

| 🌐 USD - US Dollar ▼ | 2019-05-17 🗓 | → |

XE Currency Table: USD - US Dollar

2019-05-17 09:51 UTC

All figures are live mid-market rates, which are not available to consumers and are for informational purposes only. To see the rates we quote for money transfer, please use our money transfer service.

Currency code ▲▼	Currency name ▲▼	Units per USD	USD per Unit
USD	US Dollar	1.0000000000	1.0000000000
EUR	Euro	0.8959109991	1.1161823005
GBP	British Pound	0.7836918866	1.2760116790
INR	Indian Rupee	70.1692012945	0.0142512667
AUD	Australian Dollar	1.4542404471	0.6876441939
CAD	Canadian Dollar	1.3494072423	0.7410661279
SGD	Singapore Dollar	1.3761350162	0.7266728833
CHF	Swiss Franc	1.0109205929	0.9891973781
MYR	Malaysian Ringgit	4.1781029907	0.2393430708
JPY	Japanese Yen	109.6879337489	0.0091167731
CNY	Chinese Yuan Renminbi	6.9153641128	0.1446055455
NZD	New Zealand Dollar	1.5320165040	0.6527344826

On the **Data** tab, in the **Get & Transform Data** group, click on the **From Web** button. Alternatively, on the Data tab, navigate to **Get Data > From Other Sources > From Web.**

Excel then opens the **From Web** dialog box with a URL field where you enter the address of the web page containing the data you want to import into Excel.

When you click **OK**, Excel will establish a connection to the website.

Note: If this is the first time you've connected to the website, Excel may display an **Access Web-content** dialog box with different connection options. Connect with the default which is **Anonymous**.

Once connected, Excel will display the **Navigator** screen, listing the data tables on the Selection pane on the left. When you click on a table in the Selection pane the data is displayed on the preview pane on the right.

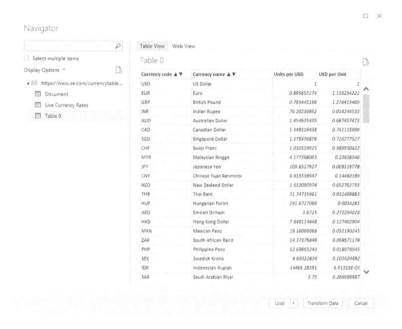

To import more than one table of data from the web page, select the **Select Multiple Items** check box and then click the checkboxes against the table names you want to import.

Once you've selected the table(s) you want to import on the page, you have the following three import options:

- The **Load** button imports the data as seen in the Navigator preview pane into your workbook (in a new worksheet).

- The **Load To** option (on the Load button's drop-down menu) opens the **Import Data** dialog box which gives you more options for how you want to import the data and where to place it. You can choose to import it as a worksheet data Table, Pivot Table, Pivot Chart, or to just establish a data connection without importing the data. You can also choose the worksheet where you want to place the data.

- The **Transform Data** button opens the data in the **Excel Power Query Editor**, which allows you to query and transform the data before importing it. For example, you may want to import only some of the data columns or filter the data with a criterion to only import a subset of the data.

After importing the data, you can manipulate and work with the data as you would with any other Excel table.

Refreshing Web Data

When working with tables imported from websites with live data, for example, financial websites like the Nasdaq or Dow Jones (while the markets are still open), you can refresh the data to reflect any changes in the data. When you import the data, Excel automatically stores information about the connection, so you just need one button click to refresh the data.

To refresh data imported from a website, on the **Data** tab, in the **Queries & Connections** group, click on the **Refresh All** button. This will automatically re-establish the connection and refresh the imported data with the latest data from the website.

3.4 Other Database Sources

Apart from Microsoft Access, the **Get Data** command on the **Data** tab also enables you to import data from a variety of database sources including:

- **From SQL Server Database:** To import data or create a connection to an SQL Server database.

- **From Analysis Services**: To import data from an SQL Server Analysis cube.

- **From SQL Server Analysis Services Database (Import)**: This is to import data from an SQL server database with the option to use an MDX or DAX query.

4. TROUBLESHOOT AND FIX FORMULA ERRORS

E rrors in simple Excel formulas are usually caused by syntax issues that can be easily fixed by correcting the syntax. For example, Excel may generate an error because a formula is missing a parenthesis and to fix the error you simply add the parenthesis to the syntax. On the other hand, a complex formula, for example, a nested formula with several levels, may not generate an error but fail to produce the expected result. This is called a logical error and they can be difficult to find.

Programming tools tend to have debuggers that can be used to step through the code to identify and fix logical errors. Fortunately, Excel 2019 provides several tools that you can use to step through complex formulas to troubleshoot and fix logical errors.

In this chapter, we will cover how to:

- Use Trace commands to trace the precedents and dependents in your formula values to identify the relationships between the results and cell references.

- Step through a nested formula one level at a time to see the evaluated result at each level.

- Use the Watch Window to display the value of a cell even when the cell is not in view.

4.1 Trace Precedents and Dependents

To help with troubleshooting your formula, you can use the **Trace Precedents** and **Trace Dependents** commands to show the relationships between the formula and any precedent or dependent cells using tracer arrows.

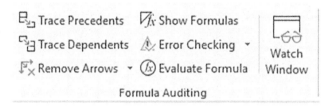

Note: The Trace commands on the Excel Ribbon are enabled by default. However, if they are disabled on your system, you need to enable them in Excel Options.

To enable Trace commands in **Excel Options**, do the following:
1. Click on **File > Options > Advanced**.
2. Scroll down to the section **Display options for this workbook** and select the workbook (if it is not already selected).
3. Under the **For objects, show** setting, select **All**.

Precedent cells are cells that are referred to by a formula in another cell. For example, if cell C2 contains the formula =A2+B2, then cells A2 and B2 are precedents to cell C2.

Dependent cells are cells that contain formulas that refer to other cells. For example, if cell C2 contains the formula =A2+B2, then cell C2 is a dependent of cells A2 and B2.

To Trace Precedents, do the following:

1. Select the cell that contains the formula that you want to trace.

2. On the **Formulas** tab, in the **Formula Auditing** group, click the **Trace Precedents** command button. This will display a tracer arrow to each cell or range that directly provides data to the active cell (cell with the formula).

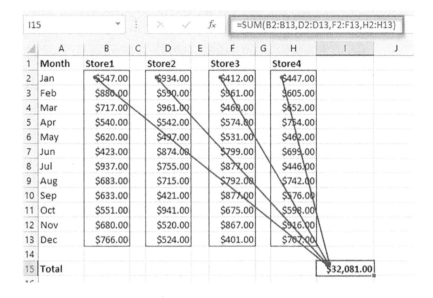

Blue arrows will show cells without errors while red arrows will show cells that cause errors. If the formula has references to a cell in another worksheet or workbook, a black arrow will point from the formula cell to a worksheet icon. If cells are referenced in other workbooks, they must be open before Excel can trace those dependencies.

3. If there are more levels of cells that provide data to the formula click on the Trace Precedents again.

To Trace Dependents, follow these steps:

1. Select the cell that contains the formula for which you want to trace dependents.

2. On the **Formulas** tab, in the **Formula Auditing** group, click **Trace Dependents**. This will display a tracer arrow to each cell that is dependent on the active cell.

3. To identify further levels of dependent cells, click Trace Dependents again.

Removing Tracer Arrows

To remove all tracer arrows, on the **Formulas** tab, in the **Formula Auditing** group, click the arrow next to **Remove Arrows**.

To remove only the precedent or dependent arrows, click on the down-arrow next to **Remove Arrows** and select **Remove Precedent Arrows** or **Remove Dependent Arrows** from the drop-down list. If you have more than one level of tracer arrows, click the button again.

4.2 Evaluate a Formula

Sometimes formulas can be complex, for example, a nested formula with several nested levels. Knowing how the formula is arriving at the final result may become difficult if there are several intermediate calculations and logical tests. Formulas that fail to produce the desired result may include logical errors that are difficult to spot at first glance.

The good news is, Excel has a tool called **Evaluate Formula** that allows you to step through a complex formula so you can see how the different levels of the formula are being evaluated, what the logical tests are doing, and the results being reached at each level. This will enable you to identify and resolve any logical errors in the syntax.

Example

In this example, we'll use the Evaluate Formula command to evaluate the following formula:

=IF(AVERAGE(E1:E8)>50,SUM(F1:F8),0)

The formula says:

   If the average of E1:E8 is greater than 50, then sum F1:F8 in cell F9.

The way nested functions work is that the inner functions are evaluated first, then the results are used as input for the outer functions. With the Evaluate Formula command, we want to see the breakdown of the results of the individual evaluations before the formula returns the final result.

The data being evaluated is shown in the image below.

=IF(AVERAGE(E1:E8)>50,SUM(F1:F8),0)

E	F	G	H
45	47		
74	30		
26	40		
39	30		
30	77		
72	79		
28	48		
68	29		
	0		

Follow the steps below to evaluate a formula:

1. Select the cell that you want to evaluate. In our example, it would be cell **F9**. Note that only one cell can be evaluated at a time.

2. On the **Formulas** tab, in the **Formula Auditing** group, click on the **Evaluate Formula** button. This will open the Evaluate Formula dialog box.

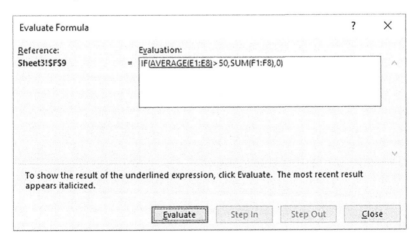

First, we see the nested formula in the **Evaluation** box with the AVERAGE and SUM functions nested within the IF function.

=IF(AVERAGE(E1:E8)>50,SUM(F1:F8),0)

3. Click **Evaluate** to examine the underlined part of the formula. The result of the evaluation will be shown in italics.

=IF(47.75>50,SUM(F1:F8),0)

The average for the values in range F1:F8 is 47.75, so AVERAGE(F1:F8) returns that figure.

Note: If the underlined part is a reference to another formula rather than a value, click **Step In** to show the other formula in the Evaluation box. Step Out takes you back to the previous cell and formula.

4. When you click on Evaluate again, you'll see the result of the logical test, which is false in this case =IF(False,SUM(F1:F8),0).

47.75 is not greater than 50, so the expression in the first argument of the IF function returns FALSE.

5. When you click on **Evaluate** again, you'll get 0 (zero) which is the final result returned by the IF function. The SUM function is not evaluated because the IF function executes the statement in the second argument only if the first argument evaluates to TRUE.

6. To go through the evaluation again, click **Restart**.

7. To end the evaluation, click **Close**.

Note: Some functions are recalculated each time the worksheet changes, hence the Evaluate Formula tool could give results different from what appears in the cell. The following functions may not work well with Evaluate Formula: RAND, OFFSET, CELL, INDIRECT, NOW, TODAY, RANDBETWEEN, INFO, SUMIF (in some scenarios).

4.3 Using the Watch Window

Another way to troubleshoot logical errors in formulas is to use the **Watch Window** toolbar in Excel. You can use the Watch Window to inspect formula calculations and results in large worksheets. With the Watch Window, you don't need to continually scroll or go to different parts of your worksheet to see different results.

The Watch Window toolbar can be moved or docked like other toolbars in Excel. For example, you can move it and dock it at the bottom of the window. To undock the Watch Window toolbar, click on the top part of it and drag it up from the docking position.

The toolbar keeps track of the following properties of a cell: workbook, worksheet, name, cell reference, the value in the cell, and formula in the cell. You can only have one watch entry per cell.

You can change data on the worksheet and view the Watch Window for how the change is affecting other cells with formulas.

Use the following steps to add a Watch item:

1. Select the cells that you want to watch.

   To select all cells with formulas on your worksheet, navigate to: **Home** tab > **Editing** group > **Find & Replace** > **Go To Special**, and then click **Formulas**.

2. On the **Formulas** tab, in the **Formula Auditing** group, click the **Watch Window** button to display the Watch Window toolbar.

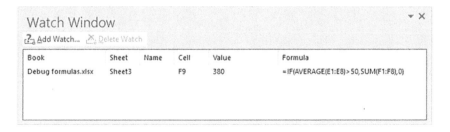

3. Click **Add Watch**.

4. Click **Add** on the **Add Watch** dialog box. Here, you can change the cell you want to add (if it is different from the one selected in step 1).

5. Move the Watch Window toolbar and dock it to the bottom, left, or right side of the Excel window. To change the width of a column, for example, the **Book** column, drag the boundary on the right side of the column heading.

6. To display the cell being referred to by an entry in the Watch Window, double-click the entry to select the cell. Note that cells that contain references to other workbooks are only displayed in the Watch Window when the referenced workbook is open.

7. To close the Watch Window toolbar, on the **Formulas** tab, in the **Formula Auditing** group, click the **Watch Window** button to toggle it off.

Removing cells from the Watch Window

1. If the Watch Window toolbar is not displayed, click the Watch Window button on the Formulas tab to display it.

2. Click the entry you want to remove to select it. To select multiple entries, press **Ctrl** and then click the entry.

3. Click **Delete Watch**.

4. To close the Watch Window toolbar, on the **Formulas** tab, in the **Formula Auditing** group, click the **Watch Window** button to toggle it off.

5. CREATE ADVANCED FORMULAS WITH FUNCTIONS

The most commonly used functions in Excel like IF, VLOOKUP, SUM, COUNT etc. were covered in detail in my *Excel 2019 Basics* book. For brevity, this book will focus on the more advanced functions that were not covered in that book. Many of these functions are relatively new to Excel and were introduced from Excel 2016 onwards. Functions are predesigned formulas, so they are tried and tested, and all you have to do is supply the inputs to get the results you need.

In this chapter, we will cover:

- Conditional statements which combine logical and aggregate functions.

- Functions that generate random numbers, especially for producing test or sample data.

- Functions to round numbers up or down.

- How to manipulate and rearrange text with functions.

- Specialised functions for financial accounting.

- Installing the Analysis ToolPak which provides more functions for carrying out complex statistical and engineering analysis.

5.1 Advanced IF Functions

In addition to the basic IF function, Excel has several conditional functions that you can use to aggregate data based on certain conditions. There are functions like IFS, SUMIF, SUMIFS, COUNTIF, AVERAGEIF etc. also referred to as advanced IF functions which we'll be covering in this section. For example, the IFS function can be used in place of convoluted nested IF statements. Several conditional aggregate functions also enable you to use one function in place of 2 or more functions.

IFS Function

The IFS function enables you to carry out multiple logical tests and execute a statement that corresponds to the first test that evaluates to TRUE. The tests need to be entered in the order in which you want the statements executed so that the right result is returned as soon as a test is passed. IFS can be used in place of nested IF statements which can quickly become too complex.

For example, the statement below has 4 nested IF functions:

=IF(D2>69,"A",IF(D2>59,"B",IF(D2>49,"C",IF(D2>39,"D","F"))))

The formula can be made much simpler with a single IFS function:

=IFS(D2>69,"A",D2>59,"B",D2>49,"C",D2>39,"D",TRUE,"F")

As you can see with the IFS variant, you don't need to worry about all the IF statements and parentheses.

Syntax

IFS(logical_test1, value_if_true1, [logical_test2, value_if_true2], [logical_test3, value_if_true3],…)

Arguments

Argument	Description
logical_test1	Required. This is the condition that is being tested. It can evaluate to TRUE or FALSE.
value_if_true1	Required. The result to be returned if *logical_test1* evaluates to TRUE.
logical_test2... logical_test127	Optional. You can add up to 127 additional tests that evaluate to TRUE or FALSE.
value_if_true2... value_if_true127	Optional. You can have up to 127 additional results to return if a logical test is true.

Note: The IFS function allows you to test up to 127 different tests. However, it is generally recommended that you do not use too many tests with IF or IFS statements. This is because the tests need to be entered in the right order and it can become too complex to update or maintain if you have too many.

Tip: As much as possible, use IFS in place of multiple nested IF statements. It is much easier to read when you have multiple conditions.

Example 1

In the example below, we use the IFS function to solve a problem we addressed earlier with nested IF statements.

In this problem, we want to assign grades to different ranges of exam scores.

Score and Grades
1. 70 or above = MERIT
2. 50 to 69 = CREDIT
3. 40 to 49 = PASS
4. less than 40 = FAIL

We derive the following formula to achieve our aim:

=IFS(A2>=70,"MERIT",A2>=50,"CREDIT", A2>=40,"PASS", A2<40,"FAIL")

| B2 | | : | × | ✓ | *fx* | =IFS(A2>=70,"MERIT",A2>=50,"CREDIT", A2>=40,"PASS", A2<40,"FAIL") |

⊿	A	B	C	D	E	F	G	H	I	J	K
1	Score	Grade									
2	70	MERIT									
3	60	CREDIT									
4	35	FAIL									
5	40	PASS									
6	85	MERIT									
7	60	CREDIT									
8											

Formula explanation

=IFS(A2>=70,"MERIT",A2>=50,"CREDIT", A2>=40,"PASS", A2<40,"FAIL")

The IFS function has been used to create four logical tests in sequential order:

A2>=70,"MERIT"
A2>=50,"CREDIT"
A2>=40,"PASS"
A2<40,"FAIL"

A2 is a reference to the score. As you can see, each score is tested against each condition in sequential order. As soon as a test is passed the corresponding grade is returned and no further testing is carried out.

Example 2

In this example, we want to set different priority levels for reordering items depending on the number of items in stock.

Priority Level:
1. 5 or less = 1
2. 10 or less = 2
3. Less than 20 = 3

The formula we use to accomplish this task is:

=IFS(A2>20,"N/A",A2<=5,1, A2<=10,2, A2<20,3)

| B2 | | : | × | ✓ | f_x | =IFS(A2>20,"N/A",A2<=5,1, A2<=10,2, A2<20,3) | | | | |

	A	B	C	D	E	F	G
1	**In stock**	**Priority Level**					
2	10	2					
3	25	N/A					
4	9	2					
5	10	2					
6	4	1					
7	10	2					
8	15	3					
9	10	2					
10	10	2					
11	5	1					
12	10	2					
13	5	1					
14	15	3					
15							

Formula explanation

=IFS(A2>20,"N/A",A2<=5,1, A2<=10,2, A2<20,3)

First, we insert a test to mark the Priority Level for any products greater than 20 as "N/A" (not applicable) as those have no Reorder priority yet. Then we carry out the tests in sequential order from the smallest value to the largest to ensure that the right corresponding value is returned as soon as a test is passed.

You can also apply conditional formatting to the results column to highlight the records with the highest priority. In this case, 1 is the highest priority.

Tip: For instructions on how to apply conditional formatting to cells, see my book Excel 2019 Basics.

SUMIF Function

The SUMIF function adds a conditional component to the SUM function, enabling you to sum up data in a range based on certain criteria.

Syntax

SUMIF(range, criteria, [sum_range])

Arguments

Argument	Description
range	Required. This is the range of cells that you want to evaluate based on the condition in *criteria*.
criteria	Required. This is the condition (or logical test) that is used to determine which cells are summed up in *range*. This can be an expression, cell reference, text, or function.
sum_range	Optional. You use this argument if you want your return value (that is the values being summed up) to be different from those used to filter the data. If this argument is omitted, then the cells specified in *range* are used.

A couple of things to take into consideration when using advanced IF functions:

- If the *criteria* argument is text or includes logical or mathematical symbols like greater than (>), for example, the whole criteria argument must be enclosed in double-quotes (""). Quotation marks are not required if *criteria* is a numeric value.

- Cells in the range argument must be numbers, names (for example, named ranges or tables), arrays, or references that contain numbers. Text values and blanks are ignored.

- You can use wildcard characters (like a question mark "?" or an asterisk "*") as the *criteria* argument. A question mark matches any single character while an asterisk matches any sequence of characters. If you want to find an actual question mark or asterisk in your data then type a tilde (~) before the character, for example, "~?".

Example 1

In this example, we're using SUMIF to only sum up values in Sales that are over $5,000.

The formula used is:

=SUMIF(A2:A11,">5000")

A14			:	✕	✓	fx	=SUMIF(A2:A11,">5000")	

	A	B	C	D	E
1	Sales	Commission			
2	$2,635	$132			
3	$7,227	$361			
4	$4,426	$221			
5	$4,774	$239			
6	$9,829	$491			
7	$20,000	$1,000			
8	$2,459	$123			
9	$11,300	$565			
10	$2,566	$128			
11	$10,894	$545			
12					
13	Report				
14	$59,250	⬅	Sum of sales over $5,000		
15	$2,963		Commission for sales over $5,000		
16					

The formula is using the criteria argument of ">5000" to filter which values will be added to the sum from the range A2:A11.

Example 2

In this example, we're using SUMIF to sum up all Commissions for sales over $5,000. We'll be using the *sum_range* argument to specify the cells we want to sum up as they are different from the cells specified in the *range* argument.

The formula we use is:

=SUMIF(A2:A11,">5000", B2:B11)

A15	▾	⋮	✕	✓	*fx*	=SUMIF(A2:A11,">5000", B2:B11)	

	A	B	C	D
1	Sales	Commission		
2	$2,635	$132		
3	$7,227	$361		
4	$4,426	$221		
5	$4,774	$239		
6	$9,829	$491		
7	$20,000	$1,000		
8	$2,459	$123		
9	$11,300	$565		
10	$2,566	$128		
11	$10,894	$545		
12				
13	Report			
14	$59,250		Sum of sales over $5,000	
15	$2,963		Commission for sales over $5,000	
16				
17				

Formula explanation

=SUMIF(A2:A11,">5000", B2:B11)

The formula is using the criteria argument ">5000" to select the values in column A (Sales) for which the corresponding values in column B (Commission) will be added to the sum. So, even though we applied the criteria to column A, the values summed up come from Column B.

SUMIFS Function

The SUMIFS function is like the SUMIF function however you can use multiple criteria to determine which cells in a range are included in the sum. SUMIFS enables you to have up to a total of 127 range/criteria pairs.

An IFS function enables you to create several range/criteria pairs used to select the data that meet the criteria. Once items that meet the criteria have been identified, the average of the corresponding values in the main range is calculated. You can have up to a maximum of 127 range/criteria pairs as you can only have 255 arguments in an Excel function.

Syntax

SUMIFS(sum_range, criteria_range1, criteria1, [criteria_range2, criteria2], ...)

Arguments

Argument	Description
Sum_range	Required. This is the range of cells you want to sum up.
Criteria_range1	Required. The range that is tested using *Criteria1*.
	Criteria_range1 and *Criteria1* are a pair where *Criteria1* is used to search *Criteria_range1* for matching values. Once items in the range are found, their corresponding values in *Sum_range* are added up.
Criteria1	Required. This is the criteria used to apply the filter on criteria1_range that selects the data subset. For example, criteria can be entered as 40, ">40", C6, "bolts", or "125".
Criteria_range2, criteria2, ...	Optional. You can have additional range/criteria pairs up to a maximum of 127 pairs in total.

Note that, the *Criteria_range* argument must reference a range that has the same number of rows and columns as the *Sum_range* argument.

Example

In the following example, we want to sum up Sales totals using 2 criteria.
1. State name
2. Orders that are 40 or more (>=40)

Formula
The following formula is derived and come of the cell references have been converted to absolute references.

Tip: To convert a cell reference to an absolute reference in the formula bar, you can enter the dollar signs manually or click on the reference within the formula (i.e. D2:D12) and press the **F4** key. This ensures that the reference will not change when the formula is copied to other cells. The difference between relative and absolute references is covered in my *Excel 2016 Basics* book.

=SUMIFS($D$2:$D$12,$B$2:$B$12,F2,$C$2:$C$12,G2)

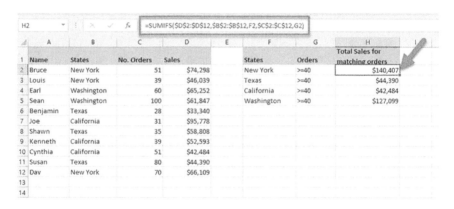

Formula explanation

=SUMIFS($D$2:$D$12,$B$2:$B$12,F2,$C$2:$C$12,G2)

- The *Sum_range* argument references the Sales column **D2:D12** (an absolute reference has been used here - **$D$2:$D$12**).

- The *Criteria_range1* is **B2:B12** (an absolute reference has also been used here - **$B$2:$B$12**)

- The Criteria1 argument is **F2**. This is a reference to the States we want to use as our criteria. A cell reference has been used for this argument to make it easier to change. This has been left as a relative reference because we want it to change relatively as we copy the formula to other cells.

- The *Criteria_range2* is **$C$2:$C$12** (in absolute reference form).

- The *Criteria2* argument is **G2** (>=40). A cell reference has been used for this argument to make it easier to change.

To sum up the Total Sales for the matching orders for each State, we enter the formula in cell **H2** and then copy it down the column.

COUNTIF Function

The COUNTIF function is a combination of the COUNT function and a conditional component. It allows you to count the number of cells in a range that meet a certain condition. For example, you can count only the values in a list of orders that exceed $1,000.

Syntax

COUNTIF(range, criteria)

Arguments

Argument	Description
range	Required. This is the group of cells that you want to count. This argument can contain numbers, a named range, or references that contain numbers.
criteria	Required. This is the condition that is used to determine which cells will be counted. This can be a cell reference, text, expression, or function. For example, you can use a number like 40, a logical comparison like ">=40", a cell reference like D10, or a word like "bolts".

Example

In this example, we're using COUNTIF to count all Sales over $5,000.

The formula we use is:

=COUNTIF(B2:B11,">5000")

C14				✗	✓	*fx*	=COUNTIF(B2:B11,">5000")	

⊿	A	B		C	D	E
1	Salesperson	Sales		Commission		
2	Bruce	$2,635		$132		
3	Louis	$7,227		$361		
4	Earl	$4,426		$221		
5	Sean	$4,774		$239		
6	Benjamin	$9,829		$491		
7	Joe	$20,000		$1,000		
8	Shawn	$2,459		$123		
9	Kenneth	$11,300		$565		
10	Cynthia	$2,566		$128		
11	Susan	$10,894		$545		
12						
13	Report					
14		Count of sales over $5,000		5		
15		Count of commissions over $200		7		
16						

The first argument is the range we want to count - **B2:B11**.

The second argument is the criteria - greater than $5,000 ("">5000"").

Note that the criterion is included in quotes because it includes a logical symbol.

Other examples

In the following examples, we have a table of data which we query with different COUNTIF formulas. The formulas, results and descriptions are shown below.

A2	▼	:	×	✓	f_x	Tea

◢	A	B	C
1	**Product**	**Orders**	
2	Tea	9	
3	Pears	20	
4	Peaches	21	
5	Pineapple	30	
6	Cherry Pie Filling	6	
7	Green Beans	10	
8	Corn	5	
9	Peas	10	
10	Tuna Fish	12	
11	Tea	5	
12	Tea	12	
13	Peaches	10	
14	Peas	2	

Formula 1	
Formula	=COUNTIF(A2:A14,"Tea")
Result	3
Description	Counts the number of cells with tea.

Formula 2	
Formula	=COUNTIF(A2:A14,A4)
Result	2
Description	Counts the number of cells with peaches (the value in A4).

Formula 3	
Formula	=COUNTIF(A2:A14,A2)+COUNTIF(A2:A14,A3)
Result	4
Description	Counts the number of teas and pears in A2:A14.

Formula 4	
Formula	=COUNTIF(B2:B14,">20")
Result	2
Description	Counts the number of values in cells B2:B14 greater than 20.

Formula 5	
Formula	=COUNTIF(B2:B14,"<>"&B7)
Result	10
Description	Counts the number of cells with a value not equal to 10 in cells B2:B14. The ampersand (&) is used for concatenation.

Formula 6	
Formula	=COUNTIF(A2:A14,"T*")
Result	4
Description	Counts the number of items starting with T in cells A2:A14.

COUNTIFS Function

COUNTIFS is an extension of the COUNTIF function that enables you to count values in multiple ranges using multiple criteria to determine what values to count.

Syntax

COUNTIFS(criteria_range1, criteria1, [criteria_range2, criteria2]...)

Arguments

Argument	Description
criteria_range1	Required. The first range you want to evaluate using the associated criteria, which is criteria1.
criteria1	Required. This is the first criteria and it pairs with criteria_range1. It could be a number, cell reference, expression, or text that define which cells will be counted. For example, criteria can be expressed as 40, ">=40", D10, "bolts", or "40".
criteria_range2, criteria2, ...	Optional. Additional ranges and criteria pairs. You can have a total of 127 range/criteria pairs.

A couple of points to take into consideration when using COUNTIFS:

- Each additional range must have the same number of rows and columns as
  criteria_range1. The ranges do not have to be adjacent to each other.

- If the criteria argument points to an empty cell, the COUNTIFS function treats the empty cell as a zero (0) value.

Example

In the following example, we want to count the number of people for each state with 40 or more orders. This problem requires us to use two criteria to evaluate two columns. We will be using the state name and ">=40" to determine which records meet our criteria.

We apply the following formula to solve the problem:

=COUNTIFS($B$2:$B$12,F2,$C$2:$C$12,G2)

H2		fx	=COUNTIFS($B$2:$B$12,F2,$C$2:$C$12,G2)					
	A	B	C	D	E	F	G	H
1	Name	State	No. Orders	Sales		States	Orders	# People
2	Bruce	New York	51	$74,298		New York	>=40	2
3	Louis	New York	39	$46,039		Texas	>=40	1
4	Earl	Washington	60	$65,252		California	>=40	1
5	Sean	Washington	100	$61,847		Washington	>=40	2
6	Benjamin	Texas	28	$33,340				
7	Joe	California	31	$95,778				
8	Shawn	Texas	35	$58,808				
9	Kenneth	California	39	$52,593				
10	Cynthia	California	51	$42,484				
11	Susan	Texas	80	$44,390				
12	Dav	New York	70	$66,109				
13								

Formula explanation:

=COUNTIFS($B$2:$B$12,F2,$C$2:$C$12,G2)

- The Criteria_range1 argument references the State column **B2:B12** (an absolute reference has been used - $B$2:$B$12).

- The Criteria1 argument is **F2**. This is a reference to the State we want to use as our criteria. A cell reference has been used for this argument to make it easier to change. This argument has left as a *relative reference* because we want it to change relative to the cell the formula is being copied to.

- The *Criteria_range2* is the *No. Orders* column (**$C$2:$C$12**). We will be using our second criteria to evaluate this column. Again, use the F4 key to make it an absolute reference.

- The *Criteria2* argument is **G2** (>=40). A cell reference has been used for this argument to make it easier to change.

We enter the formula in cell **H2** and then copy it down the column to count the number of people with orders that match the criteria for each state.

AVERAGEIF Function

AVERAGEIF is a combination of the AVERAGE function and a conditional component. AVERAGEIF returns the average (or arithmetic mean) of all the cells in a range that meet a specified condition.

Syntax

AVERAGEIF(range, criteria, [average_range])

Arguments

Argument	Description
Range	Required. A reference to one or more cells to average. This argument can include numbers, cell references, or named ranges.
Criteria	Required. This is a logical test that determines which cells are included in the average.
Average_range	Optional. The actual set of cells to average if not the cells in the *range* argument. If this argument is omitted, *range* is used.

Notes:

- Cells in *range* that contain logical values like TRUE or FALSE are ignored.

- AVERAGEIF will return an error (#DIV0!) if *range* is a blank or text value.

- If a cell in criteria is empty it is treated as a zero (0) value.

- AVERAGEIF returns the #DIV/0! error value if no cells in the range meet the criteria.

- *Average_range* does not necessarily need to be the same number of rows and columns as *range*. The cells that are averaged are determined by using the top-left cell in *average_range* as the first cell and then including cells that match the same number of rows and columns in *range*. See the examples below:

- If the *range* is A1:A10 and *average_range* is B1:B10, then the actual cells evaluated would be B1:B10.
- If *range* is A1:A10 and *average_range* is B1:B5, then the actual cells evaluated would be B1:B10.
- If *range* is A1:B5 and *average_range* is C1:C3, then the actual cells evaluated would be C1:D5.

Example

In the following example, we use the AVERAGEIF function to calculate the average exam scores for students per subject. We want to group the data by *Subject* (for example, Biology, Chemistry, Maths etc.) and average each group by *Score*.

The range we will be using to select the data - B2:B16, is different from the range we want to actually average - C2:C16.

F2			fx	=AVERAGEIF($B$2:$B$16,E2,$C$2:$C$16)	
	A	B	C	D	E	F
1	Student	Subject	Score		Average per subject	
2	Bruce	Maths	55		Maths	56.2
3	Louis	Chemistry	61		Chemistry	50.0
4	Earl	Biology	47		English	68.0
5	Sean	English	74		Biology	43.5
6	Benjamin	Maths	50			
7	Joe	Chemistry	52			
8	Shawn	Biology	40			
9	Kenneth	English	70			
10	Cynthia	Maths	45			
11	Susan	Chemistry	40			
12	John	Maths	76			
13	Bruce	English	60			
14	Louis	Maths	61			
15	Earl	Chemistry	47			
16	Kenneth	Maths	50			
17						

Formula explanation:

=AVERAGEIF($B$2:$B$16,E2,$C$2:$C$16)

- The **Range** argument references the Subject column B2:B16 (this has been set to absolute reference - **$B$2:$B$16**).

- The **Criteria** argument is **E2**. This is a reference to the subjects we want to use as our criteria. Instead of directly entering this value into the formula, a cell reference has been used to make it easier to change. This argument is a relative reference (the default) because we want the cell to change relatively as we copy the formula to other cells.

- The **Average_range** is C2:C16 (which is **$C$2:$C$16** as an absolute reference). This is the range for which we want to calculate the average of values that meet our criteria. Use the F4 key to make it an absolute reference.

We enter the formula in cell F2 to return the Maths average. Then the Fill Handle of the cell was used to copy the formula to cells F3:F5 which displays the average for the other subjects.

AVERAGEIFS Function

The AVERAGEIFS function returns the average (arithmetic mean) of all cells that meet specific criteria you specify. This function allows you to specify several pairs of criteria to select the data that is included in the average.

Syntax

AVERAGEIFS(average_range, criteria_range1, criteria1, [criteria_range2, criteria2], ...)

Arguments

Argument	Description
Average_range	Required. This is the range of cells for which you want the average calculated.
Criteria_range1	Required. The range that is evaluated using *Criteria1*. This is part of the first range/criteria pair.
Criteria1	Required. This is the criteria used to evaluate *criteria1_range* to select matching data. For example, criteria can be entered as 40, ">40", C6, "bolts", or "125".
Criteria_range2, criteria2, …	Optional. You can have additional range/criteria pairs, up to a maximum of 127 total pairs.

Example

In this example, we have a list of orders from different sales reps for several states. We want to find the average sales per state for entries that are greater than or equal to 10 orders (>=10).

We apply the following formula to solve the problem:

=AVERAGEIFS($D$2:$D$12,$B$2:$B$12,F2,$C$2:$C$12,G2)

| H2 | | | | f_x | =AVERAGEIFS($D$2:$D$12,$B$2:$B$12,F2,$C$2:$C$12,G2) | | | |

	A	B	C	D	E	F	G	H
1	Name	State	# of Orders	Sales		States	Orders	Average Sales on 10 or more orders
2	Bruce	New York	12	$74,298		New York	>=10	$70,204
3	Louis	New York	5	$46,039		Texas	>=10	$58,808
4	Earl	Washington	15	$65,252		California	>=10	$52,593
5	Sean	Washington	11	$61,847		Washington	>=10	$63,550
6	Benjamin	Texas	9	$33,340				
7	Joe	California	3	$30,000				
8	Shawn	Texas	20	$58,808				
9	Kenneth	California	12	$52,593				
10	Cynthia	California	8	$42,484				
11	Susan	Texas	2	$20,000				
12	Dav	New York	10	$66,109				

Formula explanation:

=AVERAGEIFS($D$2:$D$12,$B$2:$B$12,F2,$C$2:$C$12,G2)

- The *Average_range* argument references the Sales column D2:D12 (an absolute reference has been used - **$D$2:$D$12**). This is the column for which we want to calculate the average.

- The *Criteria_range1* is B2:B12 (an absolute reference has been used - **$B$2:$B$12**).

- The *Criteria1* argument is **F2**. This is a reference to the state we want to use as our criteria. A cell reference has been used for this argument to make it easier to change.

  This has been left as a relative reference (default) because we want it to change as we copy the formula to other cells.

- The *Criteria_range2* argument is the **# of Orders** column, C2:C12. We will be using *Criteria2* to select the orders that meet the criteria from this range. An absolute reference has been used - **$C$2:$C$12**.

- The *Criteria2* argument is cell **G2** which represents our criteria (>=10). This argument is a matching pair for *Criteria_range2*. A cell reference has been used to make it easier to update with different criteria values.

The formula is entered in cell **H2** and then the Fill Handle of the cell is used to copy the formula to H3:H5. This calculates the average for the other states.

MAXIFS, MINIFS Functions

The MAXIFS and MINIFS functions are an extension of the MAX and MIN functions to include a conditional component in their functionality. MAXIFS returns the maximum value of all cells that meet the specified criteria. MINIFS returns the minimum value of all cells that meet the specified criteria. You can specify more than one set of criteria to determine which data is selected to be part of the evaluation.

Syntax

MAXIFS

MAXIFS(max_range, criteria_range1, criteria1, [criteria_range2, criteria2], ...)

MINIFS

MINIFS(min_range, criteria_range1, criteria1, [criteria_range2, criteria2], ...)

Arguments – similar for both functions

Argument	Description
max_range (MAX function) min_range (MIN function)	Required. The actual range of cells for which we want the maximum or minimum value determined.
criteria_range1	Required. The range that is evaluated using *criteria1*. This is part of the first range/criteria pair.
criteria1	Required. This is the criteria used to determine which cells in *criteria_range1* will be used to filter the data. This can be a number, expression, or text. For example, criteria can be entered as 40, ">40", C6, "bolts", or "125".

criteria_range2, criteria2, ...	Optional. You can have additional range/criteria pairs, up to a maximum of 127 total pairs.

The max_range (or min_range) and criteria_range arguments must have the same number of rows and columns, otherwise, the function will return the #VALUE! error.

Example

In this example, we want to produce reports that show the minimum and maximums sales per state. However, we only want to evaluate entries with 10 or more orders (>=10). So, we have two criteria that we want to use to determine the data to be evaluated.

Formulas

We use the following formulas to return the desired results.

Maximum:
=MAXIFS($D$2:$D$12,$B$2:$B$12,F3,$C$2:$C$12,G3)

Minimum:
=MINIFS($D$2:$D$12,$B$2:$B$12,F10,$C$2:$C$12,G10)

Formula explanation

We have used identical cell references and criteria arguments for both functions, so they can be described together.

MAXIFS($D$2:$D$12,$B$2:$B$12,F3,$C$2:$C$12,G3)

- The first argument for both functions is a reference to the Sales column, D2:D12. This is the actual range we want to evaluate for the minimum and maximum values. An absolute reference has been used - **$D$2:$D$12**.

- The *Criteria_range1* argument is the **State** column B2:B12. This is part of the first range/criteria pair we'll use to establish our first condition. An absolute cell reference has been used - **$B$2:$B$12**.

- The *Criteria1* argument is **F2**. This is a cell reference to our first criteria, the name of the state which is "New York" in the case of cell F2. A cell reference has been used to hold the value to make it easier to change in future if we so desire. This has been left as a relative reference because we want the references to change relative to cells the formula is copied to.

- The *Criteria_range2* argument is the **# of Orders** column, C2:C12. This is part of the second range/criteria pair. An absolute reference has been used here - **$C$2:$C$12**.

- The *Criteria2* argument is cell **G2** which represents the criteria ">=10". This is part of the second range/criteria pair used to filter the data to be evaluated. A cell reference has been used to make it easier to update with different criteria values.

To display the results, we enter the MAXIFS formula in cell **H2** and use the Fill Handle of the cell to copy the formula down to **H5**. This calculates the maximum sales for the other states.

For the minimum values, we enter the MINIFS formula in cell **H10** and use the Fill Handle to copy the formula down to **H13** to calculate the minimum sales for the other states.

IFERROR Function

This function is used to trap errors in Excel formulas and return a meaningful message. It is like how errors are trapped and handled in computer code. IFERROR can trap the following error types: #VALUE!, #N/A, #DIV/0!, #REF!, #NAME?, #NUM!, or #NULL!.

Syntax

IFERROR(value, value_if_error)

Arguments

Argument	Description
value	Required. This is the argument that is checked for an error. This can be a cell reference or a formula.
value_if_error	Required. This is the value that is returned if the formula evaluates to an error.

Remarks

- If either *value* or *value_if_error* points to an empty cell, IFERROR treats it as an empty string value ("").

- If *value* is an array formula, IFERROR returns an array of results, one for each cell in the results range.

Example

In the following example, we use the IFERROR formula to trap any errors in our formula in column C and return a text message "Calculation error".

For this exercise, the FORMULATEXT function has been used in D2:D5 to reveal the formulas in columns C2:C5.

C2	▾	⋮	✕	✓	f_x	=IFERROR(B2/A2,"Calculation error")	

▲	A	B	C	D	E
1	Target	Actual Units Sold	Percentage		
2	200	35	18%	=IFERROR(B2/A2,"Calculation error")	
3	10	0	0%	=IFERROR(B3/A3,"Calculation error")	
4	120	50	42%	=IFERROR(B4/A4,"Calculation error")	
5		5	Calculation error	=IFERROR(B5/A5,"Calculation error")	
6					
7					
8					
9					

5.2 Math Functions

The mathematics functions in Excel can be found by clicking the Math & Trig command button on the Formulas tab of the Ribbon. The drop-down menu lists all the Math & Trig functions. This category of functions in Excel ranges from common arithmetic functions to complex functions used by mathematicians and engineers. Our focus here will be on functions that enable you to generate random numbers and round figures up or down.

RAND function

The RAND function generates a random decimal number between 0 and 1, for example, RAND will generate a number like 0.857519619. A new random number is generated every time the worksheet is calculated, hence, if you don't want the number to change each time the worksheet is calculated you have to keep only the value generated and not the formula.

You can enter =RAND() in the formula bar, and then press **F9** to generate a random value only without the formula entered in the cell. Alternately, you can generate numbers on another part of your worksheet and then copy and paste only the values to the target cells.

Syntax

RAND()

The RAND function has no arguments.

Example

In the example below, we use the RAND function with different combinations to generate numbers in different ranges.

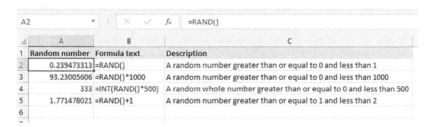

	A	B	C
1	Random number	Formula text	Description
2	0.239473313	=RAND()	A random number greater than or equal to 0 and less than 1
3	93.23005606	=RAND()*1000	A random number greater than or equal to 0 and less than 1000
4	333	=INT(RAND()*500)	A random whole number greater than or equal to 0 and less than 500
5	1.771478021	=RAND()+1	A random number greater than or equal to 1 and less than 2
6			

=RAND() - A random number greater than or equal to 0 and less than 1.

=RAND()*1000 - A random number greater than or equal to 0 and less than 1000.

=INT(RAND()*500) - A random whole number greater than or equal to 0 and less than 500.

=RAND()+1 - A random number greater than or equal to 1 and less than 2.

Tip: The RANDBETWEEN function is a much better function for generating numbers within a range of numbers, especially for a large set of random numbers.

RANDBETWEEN Function

The RANDBETWEEN function returns a random integer between two numbers you specify. This function comes in handy when you want to generate sample data between two numbers. For example, if you want to generate some sample data between 1 and 100 in several cells, you could use RANDBETWEEN to generate a random number in one cell and copy the formula over the required range.

Syntax

RANDBETWEEN(bottom, top)

Arguments

Argument	Description
Bottom	Required. The smallest integer to be returned.
Top	Required. The largest integer to be returned.

Note: The random values are regenerated each time the worksheet is recalculated. Hence, if you generate random values that you don't want to change each time the worksheet is recalculated, you need to copy only the values to another range without the formulas.

Example

In this example, we will use the RANDBETWEEN function to generate sample data for student scores between 0 and 100.

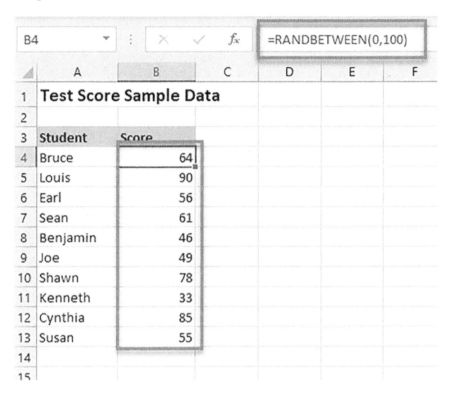

Tip: To keep only the generated values without the formula, generate the sample data in a different part of your worksheet and then copy and paste only the values into your target range. For example, if you wanted random values in cells B2:B10, generate the values using RANDBETWEEN in cells F2:F10 and then copy and paste only the values in B2:B10, then delete the values in F2:F10.

ROUND, ROUNDUP and ROUNDOWN

The ROUND function rounds a number to a specified number of digits. For example, if you have 25.4568 in cell A1 and you want to round the figure to two decimal places, when you use the formula =ROUND(A1, 2), it will return 25.46.

ROUNDUP and ROUNDOWN are similar to ROUND but as their name suggests, they round numbers in a specific direction. ROUNDUP always rounds a number up, away from zero while ROUNDOWN always rounds a number down, towards zero.

Syntax

ROUND(number, num_digits)

ROUNDUP(number, num_digits)

ROUNDDOWN(number, num_digits)

Arguments

Argument	Description
number	Required. This argument is the number that you want to round.
num_digits	Required. This is the number of decimal places to which you want to round the number.

A couple of points to take into consideration when using these three functions:

- If *num_digits* is greater than zero (that is the number of decimal places to which you want to round the number), then the number is rounded to the specified number of decimal places.

- If *num_digits* is 0 (zero), then the number is rounded to the nearest integer.

- If *num_digits* is less than 0 (zero), then the number is rounded to the left of the decimal point.

- Use the ROUNDUP function if you want to always round up (away from zero).

- Use the ROUNDDOWN function if you want to always round down (toward zero).

Examples

In the following examples, ROUND, ROUNDUP and ROUNDOWN are applied to different values to show the output. The tables below display the formula, the result, and a description of the result.

Formula	Result	Description
=ROUND(3.15, 1)	3.2	Rounds 3.15 to one decimal place.
=ROUND(4.149, 1)	4.1	Rounds 4.149 to one decimal place.
=ROUND(-2.475, 2)	-2.48	Rounds -2.475 to two decimal places.
=ROUND(57.5, -1)	60	Rounds 57.5 to one decimal place to the left of the decimal point.
=ROUND(671.3,-3)	1000	Rounds 671.3 to the nearest multiple of 1000.
=ROUND(1.78,-1)	0	Rounds 1.78 to the nearest multiple of 10.
=ROUND(-70.45,-2)	-100	Rounds -70.45 to the nearest multiple of 100.

Formula	Result	Description
=ROUNDUP(3.15, 1)	3.2	Rounds 3.15 up to one decimal place.
=ROUNDUP(4.149, 1)	5	Rounds 4.149 up to zero decimal places.
=ROUNDUP(-2.475, 2)	-2.48	Rounds -2.475 to two decimal places.
=ROUNDUP(57.5, -1)	60	Rounds 57.5 to one decimal place to the left of the decimal point.
=ROUNDUP(671.3,-2)	700	Rounds 671.3 to two decimal places to the left of the decimal point.
=ROUNDUP(1.78,0)	2	Rounds 1.78 up to zero decimal places.
=ROUND(-70.45,-2)	-100	Rounds -70.45 to the nearest multiple of 100.

Formula	Result	Description
=ROUNDDOWN(3.15, 1)	3.1	Rounds 3.15 down to one decimal place.
=ROUNDDOWN(4.149, 0)	4	Rounds 4.149 down to zero decimal places.
=ROUNDDOWN(-2.475, 2)	-2.47	Rounds -2.475 down to two decimal places.
=ROUNDDOWN(57.5, -1)	50	Rounds 57.5 down to one decimal place to the left of the decimal point.
=ROUNDDOWN(671.3,-2)	600	Rounds 671.3 down to the nearest multiple of 100.
=ROUNDDOWN(1.78,0)	1	Rounds 1.78 down to zero decimal places.
=ROUNDDOWN(-71.45,-1)	-70	Rounds -71.45 down to the nearest multiple of 10.

5.3 Manipulate Text with Functions

The text functions in Excel can be found in Excel by clicking the Text command button on the Formulas tab on the Ribbon. The drop-down menu lists all the text functions in Excel. If you work with Excel extensively, there are going to be occasions when you would need to use functions to manipulate text, especially when you work with data imported from other programs.

Tip: The **Flash Fill** command on the **Home** tab enables you to automatically perform many text-manipulation tasks for which you would previously use functions. To learn more about Flash Fill, see my book *Excel 2019 Basics*.

FIND Function

The FIND function enables you to identify the starting position of one text string within another text string. It returns the position of the first character of the text your searching for within the second text. The search is case sensitive.

Syntax

FIND(find_text, within_text, [start_num])

Arguments

Argument	Description
Find_text	Required. This is the text you want to find.
Within_text	Required. This is the text containing the text you want to find.
Start_num	Optional. This argument specifies the point, in characters, from which you want to start the search in *within_text*. The first character in *within_text* is character number 1. If you omit this argument it will start from the first character in *within_text*.

Example 1

In this example, we use the FIND function to return the position of different characters in the string "United States". As you can see from the results, the FIND function is case sensitive.

A5			fx	=FIND("S",$A$2)

	A	B	C
1	Data		
2	United States		
3			
4	Result	Formula	Explanation
5	8	=FIND("S",$A$2)	Returns the position of uppercase S in United States
6	13	=FIND("s",$A$2)	Returns the position of lowercase s in United States
7	4	=FIND("t",$A$2)	Returns the position of the first lowercase t in United States
8			
9			
10			

Example 2

The FIND function is most useful when used with another string function in Excel. For example, let's say we want to extract the first part of a reference number like NWTBGM-21. We can use FIND to locate the position of the divider and use the LEFT function to extract the part of the reference we want.

Clipboard		Font			Alignment

C2			fx	=LEFT(A2,FIND("-",A2)-1)

	A	B	C	D	E
1					
2	NWTBGM-21		NWTBGM		
3					
4					

=LEFT(A2,1,FIND("-",A2,1)-1)

FIND returns the position of "-", which is 7 in this case. We need to subtract 1 from this number to remove the divider from the part of the string we're interested in. The LEFT function then uses 6 as the starting point to return the characters in the string starting from right to left. See the section **LEFT, RIGHT Functions** in this book for more on the LEFT function.

LEFT, RIGHT Functions

The LEFT function returns the leftmost characters in a text string based on the number of characters you specify in one of its arguments. The RIGHT function returns the rightmost characters in a text string based on a number you specify.

Syntax

LEFT(text, [num_chars])

RIGHT(text,[num_chars])

Arguments

Argument	Description
Text	Required. This argument represents the text string with the characters you want to extract.
Num_chars	Optional. This is a number that specifies the number of characters you want to extract from the left (for the LEFT function) or right (for the RIGHT function).

Remarks

- If *num_chars* is larger than the length of *text*, the functions will return all characters in *text*.

- If *num_chars* is omitted, the functions return only the first character for the LEFT function and only the last character for the RIGHT function.

Example

In the example below, we use the LEFT and RIGHT functions to extract portions of text in different ways.

B2			f_x	=LEFT(A2)

	A	B	C
1	Text	Result	Formula
2	Alabama - AL	A	=LEFT(A2)
3	Alaska - AK	K	=RIGHT(A3)
4	Arizona - AZ	Arizona	=LEFT(A4,7)
5	Arkansas - AR	AR	=RIGHT(A5,2)
6	California - CA	California	=LEFT(A6,FIND("-",A6)-1)
7	Colorado - CO	Colorado	=LEFT(A7,FIND("-",A7)-1)
8	Connecticut - CT	Connecticut	=LEFT(A8,FIND("-",A8)-1)
9	Delaware - DE	DE	=RIGHT(A9,LEN(A9)-(FIND("-",A9)+1))
10	Florida - FL	FL	=RIGHT(A10,LEN(A10)-(FIND("-",A10)+1))
11	Georgia - GA	GA	=RIGHT(A11,LEN(A11)-(FIND("-",A11)+1))
12			

Formula explanations

=LEFT(A2)

This formula takes in cell A2 as the text argument and ignores the optional Num_chars argument. This returns the first character on the left of the string.

=RIGHT(A3)

This formula takes in cell A3 as the text argument and ignores the optional Num_chars argument. Hence the result it returns is the last character in the string (or first from the right).

=LEFT(A4,7)

This formula takes in cell A4 as the text argument and has 7 as the Num_chars argument. It returns "Arizona" which is 7 characters from the left of the string.

=RIGHT(A5,2)

This formula takes in cell A4 as the text argument and has 7 as the Num_chars argument. It returns "AR" which is 2 characters from the right of the string.

=LEFT(A6,FIND("-",A6)-1)

This formula takes in cell A6 as the text argument. We calculate the Num_chars argument by using the FIND function to find and return the position of the dash character (-) in the text.

We then subtract 1 from the result to return the number of characters in the text before the dash. Hence **FIND("-",A6)-1** will return 10. The result is California. This formula will work for any piece of text separated by a dash for which you want to extract the left portion.

=RIGHT(A9,LEN(A9)-(FIND("-",A9)+1))

This formula takes in cell A9 as the text argument. We calculate the Num_chars argument by first using FIND to return the position of the dash character (-) in the text. We then add 1 to move to the position of the first character after the dash (on the right).

The LEN function is used to get the length of the string as we want to subtract the number of characters returned by FIND to give us the number of characters after the dash, which is 2 in this case.

This formula will work for any piece of text separated by a dash for which you want to extract the right portion, regardless of the number of characters after the dash.

MID Function

The MID function enables you to extract a portion of a text string based on a starting position you specify and the number of characters you want to extract. The LEFT and RIGHT functions enable you to extract text from the left or the right edge of the string while MID enables you to extract text from the middle of the string. The MID function is often used with the LEN function which returns the length of a text string (that is the number of characters in the string).

Syntax

MID(text, start_num, num_chars)

Arguments

Argument	Description
Text	Required. A text string or a cell reference containing the characters you want to extract.
Start_num	Required. This is a number representing the starting position of the first character you want to extract in *text*. The first character in *text* starts with 1, the second is 2 and so on.
Num_chars	Required. This is a number that specifies the number of characters you want to extract from *text*.

Notes:

- If the start_num argument is larger than the length of the string in our text argument, MID will return an empty text ("").

- MID will return the #VALUE! error if start_num is less than 1.

- MID returns the #VALUE! error if num_chars is a negative value.

Example

The examples below demonstrate how to use the FIND and MID functions and how you can combine these functions to extract portions of text.

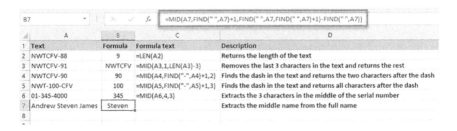

Formula explanation

The last example from the image above uses a combination of the MID and FIND functions to extract the middle name **Steven** from the full name **Andrew Steven James**.

Formula used:
=MID(A7,FIND(" ",A7)+1,FIND(" ",A7,FIND(" ",A7)+1)-FIND(" ",A7))

The first objective is to find the second space and hence where the middle name ends. This is achieved with:

FIND(" ",A2,FIND(" ",A2)+1)

The second objective is to find the first space and hence where the middle name starts. This is achieved with:

FIND(" ",A7)+1

Next, we calculate the length of the middle name by subtracting the number of characters representing the end of the name from the number of characters representing the start of the name:

FIND(" ",A2,FIND(" ",A2)+1)-FIND(" ",A7)

This is now our *num_chars* argument for the MID function.

When we put the formulas together as arguments in the MID function, we get the following formula that will extract a middle name of any length as long as it is separated by a space.

=MID(A7,FIND(" ",A7)+1,FIND(" ",A7,FIND(" ",A7)+1)-FIND(" ",A7))

The benefit of using a formula like this is that you create it once and use the Fill Handle of the first cell to copy the formula to the other cells. The formula will work for any combination of first name, middle name, and last name as long as they are separated by a space.

PROPER Function

The PROPER function capitalizes the first letter in a text string and converts all other letters in the string to lowercase letters. A text string is a continues stream of characters without spaces. Every letter after a space or punctuation character is capitalized.

Syntax

PROPER(text)

Argument	Description
Text	Required. This can be a string, a cell reference, or a formula that returns a text string that you want to partially capitalize.

Example

In the example below, we use the PROPER function to achieve the desired capitalization for a series of text strings.

=PROPER(A1)

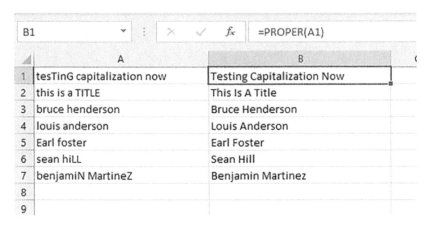

5.4 Financial Functions

The financial functions in Excel can be accessed by clicking the Financial button on the Formulas tab of the Ribbon. Most of the financial functions in Excel are specialized functions used for financial accounting so before we dive into these functions, we need to cover some financial definitions used in their arguments. Terms like PV (Present Value), FV (Future Value), PMT (Payment), and IPMT (interest payment) come up numerous times in the different financial functions.

Definitions

Annuity
An annuity is a series of regular cash payments over a certain period. For example, a mortgage or a car loan is an annuity. An investment that pays you regular dividends is also an annuity. Most of the functions we will be covering in this chapter are known as annuity functions.

PV (Present Value)
This is the present value of an investment based on a constant growth rate. It is the lump-sum amount that a series of future payments is worth right now.

FV (Future Value)
This is the future value of an investment based on a constant rate of growth. For example, let's say you want to save $25,000 to pay for a project in 20 years, hence, $25,000 is the future value. To calculate how much you need to save monthly, you'll also need to factor in an assumed interest rate over the period.

PMT (Payment)
This is the payment made for each period in the annuity. Usually, the payment includes the principal plus interest without any other fees, and it is set over the life of the annuity. For example, a $100,000 mortgage over 25 years at 3% interest would have monthly payments of $474. You would enter -474 into the formula as the *pmt*.

RATE

This is the interest rate per period. For example, if you get a loan at a 6% annual interest rate and make monthly payments, your interest rate per month would be 6%/12.

NPER (Number of periods)

This is the total number of payment periods in the life of the annuity i.e. the term. For example, if you get a 3-year loan and make monthly payments, your loan will have 3*12 periods. Hence, you would enter 3*12 into the formula for the *nper* argument.

Note: The FA, PV, and PMT arguments can be positive or negative values depending on whether you are paying out money or receiving money. If you are paying out money, then the figures will be negative; if you are receiving money then the figures will be positive.

PV Function

The PV function calculates the present value of an investment (or a loan), assuming a constant interest rate. This is the amount that a series of future payments is currently worth. You can use PV with regular payments (such as a mortgage or other loan), periodic payments, or the future value of a lump sum paid now.

Syntax

PV(rate, nper, pmt, [fv], [type])

Arguments

Please see the Definitions section above for a more detailed description of these arguments.

Arguments	Description
Rate	Required. This is the interest rate per period.
Nper	Required. The total number of payment periods in an annuity i.e. the term.
Pmt	Required. This is the payment made for each period in the annuity.
	If you omit *pmt*, you must include the *fv* argument.
Fv	Optional. This is the future value of an investment based on an assumed rate of growth.
	If you omit fv, it is assumed to be 0 (zero), for example, the future value of a loan is 0. If you omit fv then you must include the pmt argument.
Type	Optional. This argument is 0 or 1 and indicates when payments are due.
	0 or omitted = at the end of the period.
	1 = at the beginning of the period.

Some points to take into consideration when using annuity functions:

- You always need to express the rate argument in the same units as the nper argument. For example, say you have monthly payments on a three-year loan at 5% annual interest. If you use 5%/12 for *rate*, you must use 3*12 for *nper*. If the payments on the same loan are being made annually, then you would use 5% for rate and 3 for nper.

- In annuity functions, the cash paid out (like a payment to savings) is represented by a negative number. The cash you receive (like a dividend payment) is represented by a positive number. For example, a $500 deposit to the bank would be represented by the argument - 500 if you are the depositor, and by the argument 500 if you are the bank.

Example

In the example below, we use the PV formula to calculate:

1. The present value of a $500 monthly payment over 25 years at a rate of 1.5% interest.
2. The present value of the lump sum now needed to create $20,000 in 10 years at a rate of 3.5% interest.

E2					f_x	=PV(A2/12,B2*12,C2)	
	A	B	C	D	E	F	
1	Annual Interest Rate	Term (years)	Payment	Future Value	Present Value	Formula	
2	1.50%	25	($500.00)		$125,019.90	=PV(A2/12,B2*12,C2)	
3	3.50%	10		$20,000.00	($14,100.94)	=PV(A3/12,B3*12,,D3)	
4							
5							
6							

Explanation of Formulas:

=PV(A2/12,B2*12,C2)

As you've probably noticed, the units for *rate* and *nper* have been kept consistent by specifying them in monthly terms, A2/12 and B2*12. The payment (pmt) has been entered in the worksheet as a negative value as this is money being paid out.

=PV(A3/12,B3*12,,D3)

The present value is a negative number as it shows the amount of cash that needs to be invested today (paid out) to generate the future value of $20,000 in 10 years at a rate of 3.5% interest.

FV Function

The FV function calculates the future value (at a specified date in the future) of an investment based on a constant interest rate. You can use FV to calculate the future value of regular payments, periodic payments, or a single lump-sum payment.

Syntax

FV(rate,nper,pmt,[pv],[type])

Arguments

Please see the Definitions section of this chapter for more a detailed description of these arguments.

Arguments	Description
Rate	Required. This is the interest rate per period.
Nper	Required. The total number of payment periods in an annuity i.e. the term.
Pmt	Required. This is the payment made for each period in the annuity.
	If you omit pmt, you must include pv.
Pv	Optional. This is the present value of an investment based on a constant growth rate.
	If you omit pv, it is assumed to be 0 (zero) and you must include pmt.
Type	Optional. The *type* is 0 or 1 and it indicates when payments are due.
	0 (or omitted) = at the end of the period.
	1 = at the beginning of the period.

Example

In the example below, we use the FV function to calculate:

1. The future value of a monthly payment of $200 over 10 months at an interest of 6% per annum.

2. The future value of a lump sum of $1,000 plus 12 monthly payments of $100, at an interest rate of 6%.

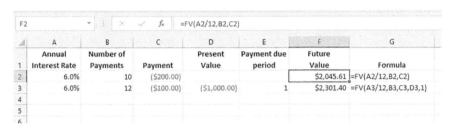

F2			×	✓	fx	=FV(A2/12,B2,C2)		
	A	B	C		D	E	F	G
	Annual	Number of			Present	Payment due	Future	
1	Interest Rate	Payments	Payment		Value	period	Value	Formula
2	6.0%	10	($200.00)				$2,045.61	=FV(A2/12,B2,C2)
3	6.0%	12	($100.00)		($1,000.00)		1	$2,301.40 =FV(A3/12,B3,C3,D3,1)
4								
5								
6								

Explanation of Formulas:

=FV(A2/12,B2,C2)

Note that the *rate* argument has been divided by 12 to represent monthly payments. The *pmt* argument is a negative value (C2) as this is money being paid out.

=FV(A3/12,B3,C3,D3,1)

This formula has the pmt argument as well as the optional pv argument which represents the present value of the investment. The payment due period is 1 which means the payment starts at the beginning of the period.

NPV Function

The NPV function calculates the net present value which is the present value of cash inflows and cash outflows over a period. It calculates the present value of an investment by applying a discount rate and a series of future payments that may be income (positive values) or payments/losses (negative values).

Syntax

NPV(rate,value1,[value2],...)

Arguments

Argument	Description
Rate	Required. This is the percentage rate of discount over the length of the investment.
Value1	Required. This represents either a payment/loss (negative value) or income (positive value).
value2, ...	Optional: You can have additional values representing payments and income up to a total of 254 value arguments.
	The length of time between these payments must be equally spaced and occur at the end of each period.

Some points to note when using this function:

- The rate argument in the function might represent the rate of inflation or the interest rate that you might get from an alternative form of investment, for example, a high-yield savings account.

- The value arguments represent the projected income (or loss) values over the period of the investment.

- Ensure you enter the payment and income values in the correct order because NPV uses the order of the value arguments to interpret the order of cash flows.

- The NPV investment begins one period before the date of the first cash flow (value1) and ends with the last cash flow in the list of value arguments. If the first cash flow happens at the beginning of the period, you must add it to the result of the NPV function and not include it as one of its value arguments.

- The main difference between NPV and PV is that with PV, the cash flows can start at the beginning or end of the period while for NPV the cash flows start at the beginning of the period. Also, PV has the same cash flow amount throughout the investment while NPV can have different cash flow amounts.

- Arguments that are not numbers are ignored.

Example

In the example below, we are calculating the net present value of an initial investment of $50,000 over the course of five years, considering an annual discount rate of 2.5 per cent.

Formula explanation

=NPV(I4,C4:G4)+B4

In the figure above, Year 1 of the investment shows a loss of $1,000, hence, this has been entered as a negative value. The other years of the investment (years two to five) returned a profit, so these were entered as positive values.

The function uses two arguments, the *rate* and *value1*, which references cells C4:G4. The initial investment is added to the result returned by the function rather than being an argument in the function.

The result shows the net present value of the investment over five years is:

$46,727.78.

PMT Function

The PMT function calculates the payment for a loan on regular payments and a constant interest rate over a period. The PMT function is often used to calculate the repayment of a mortgage with a fixed interest rate.

Syntax

PMT(rate, nper, pv, [fv], [type])

Arguments

Arguments	Description
Rate	Required. This is the interest rate per period.
Nper	Required. This is the total number of payment periods in an annuity i.e. the term.
Pv	Required. This is the present value of a principal or a series of future payments.
Fv	Optional. This is the future value of an investment based on an assumed rate of growth. If you omit fv, it is assumed to be 0 (zero), i.e. the future value of a loan is 0.
Type	Optional. This argument is 0 or 1 and indicates when payments are due. 0 (or omitted) = at the end of the period. 1 = at the beginning of the period.

Some points to take into consideration when using annuity functions:

- The payment returned by PMT is for the principal and interest. It does not include taxes, reserve payments, or other fees they may be associated with loans.

- You always need to express the *rate* argument in the same units as the *nper* argument. For example, say you have monthly payments on a three-year loan at 5% annual interest. If you use 5%/12 for *rate*, you must use 3*12 for *nper*. If the payments on the same loan are being made annually, then you would use 5% for rate and 3 for nper.

Tip: To calculate the total amount paid over the duration of the loan, simply multiply the value returned by PMT by the number of payments (nper).

Example

In the example below, we calculate the PMT for two loans:

1. A $10,000 loan over 12 payments at 8.0 percent interest.

2. A $10,000 loan over 60 payments at 4.9 percent interest.

	D2				f_x	=PMT(A2/12,B2,C2)		
	A	B	C	D		E		F
1	Annual Interest Rate	Number of payments	Amount of loan	PMT		Formula		
2	8.0%	12	$10,000.00	($869.88)		=PMT(A2/12,B2,C2)		
3	4.9%	60	$10,000.00	($188.25)		=PMT(A3/12,B3,C3)		
4								
5								

Formula explanation

=PMT(A2/12,B2,C2)

The rate argument is a reference to cell A2 divided by 12, to represent the interest rate in monthly terms as nper (cell B2) is also specified in monthly terms. The pv argument takes in C2, which is the present value of the loan $10,000.

Answer: ($869.88)

=PMT(A3/12,B3,C3)

This formula is also for a loan of $10,000, however, the nper is 60 and the rate is 4.9 percent.

Answer: ($188.25)

Installing the Analysis ToolPak

The Excel Analysis ToolPak is an add-on that you can install that enables you to carry out complex statistical or engineering analyses. You can save a lot of time as you simply provide the data and parameters, and the tool uses the appropriate engineering or statistical functions to calculate and display the results in output tables. Some of the tools even generate charts in addition to output tables.

You can only use the data analysis functions on one worksheet at a time. When you carry out data analysis on a group of worksheets at the same time, results will appear on the first worksheet and empty tables will appear on the remaining worksheets. To carry out the data analysis on the rest of the worksheets, you'll need to recalculate the analysis tool for each worksheet.

Follow these steps to install the Analysis ToolPak:

1. Click on **File** > **Excel Options** (or press Alt+FT to directly open the Excel Options dialog box), and then click on **Add-Ins**.

   The Add-Ins tab lists all the names, locations, and types of the add-ins currently available to you in Excel.

2. In the **Manage box** (at the bottom of the Add-ins tab), select **Excel Add-ins** and then click **Go**.

   If you're on a Mac, in the file menu go to **Tools** > **Excel Add-ins**.

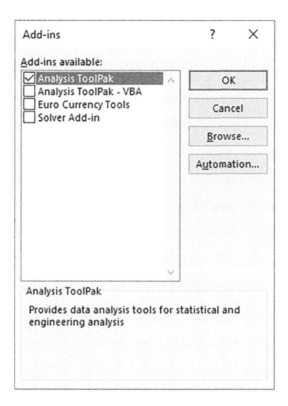

3. In the **Add-Ins** dialog box, select the **Analysis ToolPak** check box, and then click on **OK**.

4. To access the Analysis ToolPak tools on the Excel Ribbon, click on the **Data** tab, then in the **Analysis** group, click on the **Data Analysis** button.

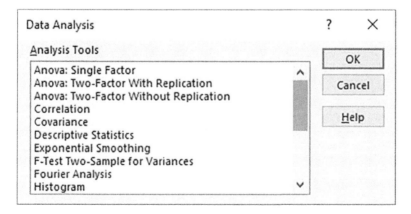

Notes:

- If Analysis ToolPak is not listed in the Add-Ins box, click Browse to find it on your computer. You may get a prompt saying that the Analysis ToolPak is not currently installed on your computer, click **Yes** to install it.

- (Optional) To include the Visual Basic for Application (VBA) functions for the Analysis ToolPak, you can also select the **Analysis ToolPak - VBA** check box. This is only required if you intend to use VBA code in your data analysis.

6. USE MACROS TO AUTOMATE EXCEL TASKS

Macros enable you to automate pretty much any task you can carry out in Excel. You can use Excel's macro recorder to record tasks that you perform routinely. Macros enable you to do the work faster as Excel can play back keystrokes and mouse actions much faster than when you perform them manually. Also, macros ensure that you carry out the tasks the same way each time, which reduces the likelihood of errors.

Excel uses the Visual Basic for Applications (VBA) programming language to record all the commands and keystrokes that you make when you're recording the macro. VBA is a programming language developed and used primarily for Microsoft Office programs like Access, Word, Excel, PowerPoint etc. You don't need to have any knowledge of VBA to record and use macros in Excel, however, you have the option of using the Visual Basic Editor to view and edit your macros after recording them, if necessary.

In this chapter, we will cover:

- How to record and run macros in Excel.
- Add macro command buttons on the Ribbon and Quick Access Toolbar.
- Assign a macro to a graphics object in your worksheet.
- Macro security, including the Trust Center and Trusted Locations.
- How to view and edit your macros in the Visual Basic editor.

There are two ways you can create a macro in Excel 2019:

1. You can use Excel's macro recorder to record your actions as you perform a task in the worksheet.

2. Use the VBA editor to directly write the code that performs the task. Visual Basic programming is outside scope of this book, but we will briefly look at the code editor.

Whichever method you use, Excel will create a special code module that holds the actions and instructions recorded in the macro. These are stored as Visual Basic code. In fact, one way to create VBA code for Excel is to simply start the recorder and manually perform the task for which you want to write code. Then you open the macro in the VBA editor and put the finishing touches to the code. This is how developers can quickly create code that automates Excel.

The macro that you create can be stored in the following locations:

- The current workbook.

- A new workbook.

- The globally available Personal Macro Workbook called PERSONAL.XLSB that is stored in a folder called XLSTART in the AppData folder for Excel on your PC.

When you record a macro and store it in the **Personal Macro Workbook**, you can run that macro from any open workbook. Macros that are saved as part of the current workbook can only be run from within that workbook.

When recording a macro, you get to choose where you want to save the macro, what to name the macro, and what shortcut keystrokes to assign the macro.

When assigning a shortcut keystroke to run the macro, you can assign the **Ctrl** key plus a letter from A-Z, for example, Ctrl+M, or Ctrl+Shift and a letter from A-Z, for example, Ctrl+Shift+M.

There are some shortcut keystrokes you can't assign, for example, Ctrl+ (any number) or Ctrl+ (a punctuation mark). Also, you should avoid using known Windows shortcut keys like Ctrl+C or Ctrl+V (that is the shortcut keys for copy and paste).

6.1 How to Start the Macro Recorder

There are three ways you can start the macro recorder in Excel:

1. On the Excel Status bar, click the **Record Macro** button (bottom left of the screen, next to the Ready indicator). Having the Record Macro button on the status bar is convenient because it means you don't have to switch from your current tab on the Ribbon to start and stop the recording.

2. On the View tab, click **Macros** and select **Record Macro** from the drop-down menu.

3. On the **Developer** tab, click the **Record Macro** command button. If you don't have the **Developer tab** on your Ribbon, follow the steps below to add it to the Ribbon:

    i. Click **File > Options** and then click the **Customize Ribbon** tab on the **Excel Options** dialog box.

    ii. Excel opens the **Customize the Ribbon** pane in the Excel Options dialog box.

    iii. On the right side of the Customize the Ribbon pane, you'll see the **Main Tabs** list. Check the **Developer** check box and then click **OK**.

Tip: Another way to open the **Customize the Ribbon** pane is to right-click anywhere on the Ribbon (below the tabs) and select **Customize the Ribbon** from the pop-up menu. This will take you directly to the **Customize the**

Ribbon pane in Excel Options. For more on customizing the Excel 2019 Ribbon, see my Excel 2019 Basics book.

On the **View** tab of the Ribbon, the **Macros** button has three options on its drop-down list (you can also find these options as command buttons in the Code group in the Developer tab):

- **View Macros**: This opens the **Macro** dialog box which enables you to select and run a macro that has already been recorded. You can also choose to edit macros from here.

- **Record Macro**: This opens the **Record Macro** dialog box which allows you to define settings for the macro you want to record and then start the macro recorder.

- **Use Relative References**: This setting, which you can turn on before recording a macro, uses relative cell references when recording macros. Using relative cell references makes the macro more versatile because it enables you to run it anywhere on the worksheet rather than where it was originally recorded.

6.2 Recording a Macro

In the following example, we'll walk through recording a macro that carries out the following tasks:

- Enters the text "Microsoft Excel 2019"
- Increases the font to 14 points
- Bolds the text
- Autofits the column width so that the text does not flow into other columns

To start recording the macro, do the following:

1. Open an Excel workbook and a blank worksheet. On the **View** tab, click the drop-down button of the **Macros** button (not the command button itself), then select **Use Relative References** from the menu.

2. On the **View** tab, click the drop-down button of the **Macros** button and click **Record Macro**. This will open the **Records Macro** dialog box.

Record Macro	?	✕

Macro name:

> MyMacro

Shortcut key:

Ctrl+ ☐

Store macro in:

> Personal Macro Workbook ⌄

Description:

> |

| OK | Cancel |

3. In the **Macro Name** field, enter the name of the macro, for example, Macro4.

4. For the **Shortcut key**, hold down the Shift key and press M. This will enter Ctrl+Shift+M for the shortcut key. This is the keystroke that you can use to run the macro. You can use other key combinations but avoid using popular Windows shortcut keys.

   Note: The shortcut key is optional, and you don't necessarily need to assign one to every macro you create.

5. In the **Store macro in** drop-down list, select **Personal Macro Workbook**. This ensures that the macro is saved in the global PERSONAL.XLSB workbook and not the current workbook.

6. In the **Description** box, you can enter a brief description of the macro. This is optional but if you're creating a lot of macros it would be a good idea to enter a description for each macro to make maintaining the macros easier.

7. When you're done, click **OK** to start recording.

The Record Macro box is closed. On the status bar, next to Ready, you'll see a small square button which is the indicator that the macro recorder is currently running.

Next, we'll perform the Excel tasks we'll be recording.

8. On the Excel Ribbon, click on the **Home** tab then click in cell **A1**.

9. Type *"Microsoft Excel 2019"* in cell A1 and click the **Enter** button (this is a checkmark next to the formula bar).

10. On the **Home** tab, change the font size to 14 and make the text bold.

11. On the **Home** tab, in the **Cells** group, click the drop-down button of the **Format** command button, then select **Autofit Column Width** from the drop-down menu. This will increase the size of the column to fit the text.

12. On the status bar, to the immediate right of **Ready**, you'll see a square button (which is the Record Macro/Stop Recording button). Click that button to stop recording the macro.

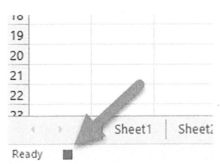

With that, your macro recording has been completed. Next, we'll run the macro.

6.3 Running a Macro

After recording a macro, there are three ways you can run it:

- On the **View** tab, click the drop-down button on the **Macros** button and select **View Macros**.

- On the **Developer** tab, in the **Code** group, click the **Macros** button.

- You can also use the **Alt+F8** shortcut keystroke to open the **Macro** dialog box.

Excel opens the **Macro** dialog box which has a list of all the macros you have created in the macro name list box.

To run the macro, click the macro name on the list and click the **Run** button.

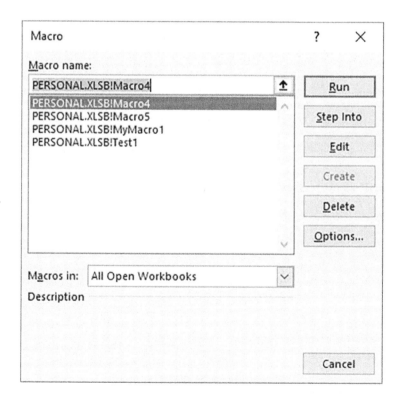

Tip: If you assigned a shortcut keystroke to the macro, for example, Ctrl+Shift+M, you can just press those keys to automatically run the macro without needing to open the Macro dialog box.

It is best to test a macro in a new worksheet (or a different range in the current worksheet) as you want to see if the macro replicates the actions you performed when recording it.

The macro recorder uses absolute references by default, which means that it will store specific cell references as part of the instructions. For example, if the macro was recorded in range A2:A5 in one worksheet, then when running in any worksheet, it will only perform the tasks in that range.

If you want the macro to perform the tasks in any range in a worksheet, you need to enable the **Use Relative Reference** setting on the **View** or **Developer** tabs of the Ribbon before you start recording the macro. With the reference type set to Relative, the macro will perform the actions relative to the active cell when the macro was started.

If you run the macro in a worksheet with existing data, there is a risk that the macro will overwrite your existing data or formatting. To ensure that you don't mistakenly overwrite data, always test the macro in a new worksheet. Only run the macro against actual data when you're satisfied that the macro is working as it should. For example, you may create a macro that adds formatting to existing data. In such cases, ensure you test the macro first against test copies of the data before running it against your live data.

6.4 Add a Macro Button to the Ribbon

To assign a macro to a custom command button, right-click anywhere on the ribbon, and select **Customize the Ribbon...** from the pop-up menu.

This will open **Customize the Ribbon** pane of the **Excel Options** dialog box.

On the **Customize the Ribbon** pane, you have two list boxes. On the right, you have the list box that shows your current tabs - **Main Tabs**. On the left, you have the command buttons that you can add to the ribbon. To expand a group in the **Main Tabs** list box, click on the plus sign (+) to the left of an item. To collapse a group, click on the minus sign (-).

Note: You cannot add or remove the default commands on the ribbon, but you can uncheck them on the list to prevent them from being displayed. Also, you cannot add command buttons to the default groups. You must create a new group to add a new command button to an existing tab.

Creating a New Custom Group

You can add the macro button to a new custom group in one of the default tabs on the Ribbon or to a new custom tab you have created for your macro buttons. We'll go through creating a new tab and then adding a command button to it.

1. To create a **new tab**, click the **New Tab** button at the bottom of the Main Tabs list box. Inside the tab, you must create at least one group before you can add a command button from the left side of the screen.

2. To give the tab a display name, select the **New Tab (Custom)** item and click the **Rename** button at the bottom of the Main Tabs list box. Enter your preferred name for the tab in the **Rename** dialog box and click **OK.**

3. You can use the arrow buttons to the right of the Main Tabs list box to move your new tab item up or down the list, depending on where you want to place it.

4. To create a new **custom group**, select the tab in which you want to create the group. This could be one of the default tabs, for example, **Home,** or the new one you've created. Click on the **New Group** button (at the bottom of the screen, under the Main Tabs list box). This will create a new group within the currently selected tab.

5. To create a display name for the group, select the **New Group (Custom)** item and click the **Rename** button. Enter your preferred name, for example, *MyMacros* in the **Rename** dialog box and click **OK.**

You now have a custom group in which you can add your macro command buttons.

Follow the steps below to add a macro command button to the new custom group:

1. Select your custom group in the **Main Tabs** list box.

2. Click the **Choose commands from** drop-down list box (on the left of the dialog box) and select **Macros** from the drop-down list. In the list box on the left, you'll see a list of macros created in the current workbook and saved in the PERSONAL.XLSB workbook.

3. Select the macro name that you want to add to your custom group in the list box on the left, then click the **Add** button to add the macro command to the new custom group in the list box on the right.

   Note: If you mistakenly added the wrong command, you could select it in the list box on the right and click the **Remove** button to remove it.

4. Click **OK** on the Excel Options dialog box to confirm the change.

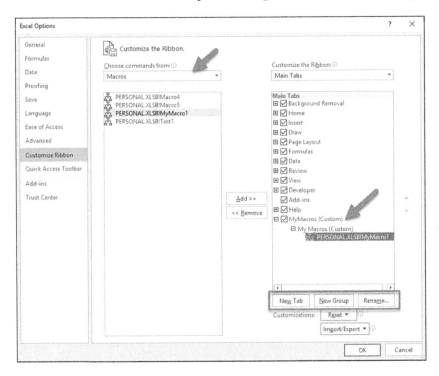

After adding the macro, the name of the macro appears on a button with a generic icon (a program diagram chart). When you click on the button it will run the macro.

6.5 Assign a Macro to a Button on the Quick Access Toolbar

Follow the steps below to add a custom macro button to the Quick Access Toolbar:

1. Click the **Customize Quick Access Toolbar** button at the end of the Quick Access toolbar. From the drop-down menu, click **More Commands**. This opens the **Customize the Quick Access Toolbar** pane in Excel Options.

2. Click the **Choose commands from** drop-down list box and select Macros from the drop-down list. In the list box on the left of the dialog box, you'll see a list of macros created in the current workbook and those saved in the PERSONAL.XLSB workbook.

3. In the list box on the left, select the macro name that you want to add to a custom button on the Quick Access Toolbar. Then click the **Add** button to add the macro command to the list on the right of the dialog box.

   Note: If you mistakenly added the wrong command, you could select it in the list on the right box and click the **Remove** button to remove it.

4. Click **OK** on the Excel Options dialog box to confirm the change.

A custom button with a generic macro icon will appear on the Quick Access Toolbar. A mouseover the button will display the name of the macro assigned to it. To run the macro, click the button.

6.6 Assign a Macro to a Graphic Object

You can assign macros to the graphic objects that you've inserted in your worksheet, including Pictures, Shapes, Icons that you can insert using **Insert > Illustrations**. You can also assign macros to graphic objects that you have drawn using tools on the **Draw** tab.

To assign a macro to a graphic object, do the following:

1. Insert the graphic object in the worksheet area, for the example, an icon from **Insert** tab > **Illustrations** > **Icons**.

2. Right-click the object and then click the **Assign Macro** option from its shortcut menu.

3. In the **Assign Macro** dialog box, select the macro name from the **Macro name** list box and click **OK**.

After you've assigned the macro to the graphic object, whenever you mouseover it, the mouse pointer changes to a hand with a pointing index finger, indicating that you can click it to run the macro.

6.7 Macro Security

Excel 2019 uses an authentication system called Microsoft Authenticode to digitally sign macro projects or add-ins created with Visual Basic for Applications. The macros you create locally on your computer are automatically authenticated so when you run them on your computer, Excel does not display a security alert.

For macros from an external source, the developer can acquire a certificate issued by a reputable authority or a trusted publisher. In such cases, Excel will run the macro if it can verify that it is from a trusted source.

If Excel cannot verify the digital signature of a macro from an external source because it perhaps doesn't have one, a security alert is displayed in the message bar (below the Excel Ribbon). This alert gives you the option to enable the macro or to ignore it. You can click the **Enable Content** button to run the macro if you trust the source and you're sure that the macro poses no security threat to your computer.

If you try to create a macro in an Excel workbook that was saved as an XLSX file, Excel will display a message on the message bar prompting you to save the workbook as a macro-enabled file first. When you get this message, click the **Save As** button on the message bar, and select the **Excel Macro-Enabled Workbook (*.xlsm)** file type from the filter list.

File type	File extension
Excel Workbook	xlsx
Excel Macro-Enabled Workbook	xlsm

If you choose to save the macro to the **Personal Macro Workbook**, it will be saved in the PERSONAL.XLSB file, which is an Excel Binary Workbook in the XLSTART folder. In this case, you'll not need to save your workbook as a macro-enabled workbook.

When creating a macro for use on your computer, as much as possible, you want to store the macro in the **Personal Macro Workbook.** This means the macro will be global and will work in any workbook on your computer. It also means that you don't need to convert your workbooks to macro-enabled files. Only use a macro-enabled workbook if there is a specific reason to do so, for example, you want to distribute the file to other people.

Trust Center Macro Settings

Microsoft Office security and privacy settings are located in the **Trust Center**. The Macro Settings tab of the Trust Center contains the macro security settings for your computer. Macro security is important to protect your computer against the threat of malicious code that can be inserted in Microsoft Office macros.

You can access the **Macro Settings** in the Trust Center in the following ways:

- On the **Developer** tab, in the **Code** group, click the **Macro Security** button. This will open the **Macro Settings** pane of the Trust Center dialog box.

- On the Ribbon, click the **File** tab and then click **Options** > **Trust Center** > **Trust Centre Settings** > **Macro Settings**.

By default, Excel 2019 disables all macros from external sources with a security alert on the message bar, giving you the option to enable the macro or ignore it. This is the default setting when you install Excel, but there are other security options from which you can choose.

You can also select one of these options in Macro Settings:

- **Disable all macros without notification**: This automatically disables macros in your computer. This setting means no macros will run on your computer and you'll not get a security alert giving you the option to run the macro. This option is useful for shared computers, for example, where you don't want anyone using the computer to run macros.

- **Disable all macros with notification**: This option is the default. All macros from external sources are disabled with a security alert showing on the message bar. With this option, you have to specifically choose to enable the macro before it can run.

- **Disable all macros except digitally signed macros**: This option disables all macros apart from the digitally signed macros from publishers that you have added to your **Trusted Publishers** in the

Trust Center. When you have this option selected and you get a macro from a publisher that's not in your Trusted Publishers list, you will get an alert in the message bar with a **Trust All Documents from this Publisher** button that you can click to add them to the to your trusted publishers.

- **Enable all macros (not recommended; potentially dangerous code can run):** This option enables all macros without any notifications or security alerts, even those macros that are not digitally signed or authenticated. As stated in its label, this option is not recommended because you can inadvertently run malicious code that corrupts your data or damages your computer.

Trusted Locations

The **Trusted Locations** tab of the Trust Center dialog box enables you to add, remove or modify trusted locations. If you are receiving macros from an external source that you need to run on your computer without alerts, then you need to place them in a trusted location on your computer. In doing so, Excel knows that these files are safe, and you are not prompted with security alerts when you open them.

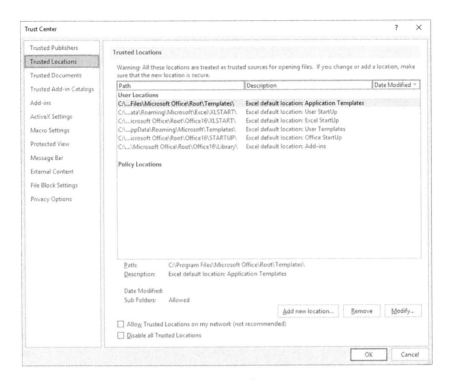

You can use the following options to change Trusted Locations settings:

- **Add new location**: To add a new trusted location, click the **Add new location** button at the bottom of the screen. On the **Microsoft Office Trusted Location** dialog box, click on the **Browse** button and navigate to the folder that you want to add to the list of trusted locations. After selecting the folder, click **OK** on the Browse dialog box, and **OK** again on the **Microsoft Office Trusted Location** dialog box to confirm the entry.

  This will add in a new trusted location on your computer and you can store any externally created macro-enabled files in that folder.

- **Allow trusted locations on my network (not recommended)**: Click this option if you want to add folders on your network to your trusted locations. As indicated by the label, this is not recommended by Microsoft as you cannot entirely trust the safety of external locations. However, if you're working on a shared network drive that you trust, and that is the only way you can collaborate with others, then this may be an option for sharing macro-enabled files. Only use as a last option.

- **Disable all trusted locations**: Check this box if you want to immediately disable all trusted locations. This means macros in these locations would not run and only the macros that are digitally signed and recognised as trustworthy by Excel will run on your computer.

Note: The macro-enabled worksheets you create locally on your computer do not need to be stored in a trusted location to run on your computer. This is because they're automatically digitally authenticated by Excel.

6.8 Editing Recorded Macros

As mentioned earlier in this chapter, the macros recorded in Excel are stored as Visual Basic for Applications code instructions.

Visual Basic for Applications (VBA) programming is outside the scope of this book. However, being able to view the source code for your macro may help you identify and fix simple errors or make small changes. Often times, editing the macro in the Visual Basic Editor to change the way it behaves is more expedient than having to record the macro again.

Even if you have no programming skills, you may still be able to identify errors and make small changes, for example, spelling errors in the text, errors in the values, or errors in formulas. You don't need programming skills to make simple changes like these. Also, you may see something out of place in the code that helps you to avoid the error if you choose to re-record the macro.

Unhiding the Personal Macro Workbook

If the macro you want to edit is stored in your Personal Macro Workbook, you must unhide this workbook before you edit it in the Visual Basic Editor.

Follow the steps below to unhide the Personal Macro Workbook:

1. On the **View** tab, click the **Unhide** command button.

Excel displays the **Unhide** dialog box showing the PERSONAL.XLSB workbook in the Unhide Workbook list.

2.   Select PERSONAL.XLSB in the list box and click on **OK** to unhide the workbook.

With the Personal Macro Workbook unhidden, you can now edit its macros in the Visual Basic Editor.

Editing the Macro in the Visual Basic Editor

Follow the steps below to open a macro for editing in the Visual Basic Editor:

1.   On the **View** tab, click the **Macros** command button then the **View Macros** option.

     This opens the **Macro** dialog box showing the names of the macros that you've created in the workbook, and your Personal Macro Workbook.

2.   In the **Macro Name** list box, select the macro name that you want to edit and then click the **Edit** button.

Excel will display the macro in the Visual Basic Editor.

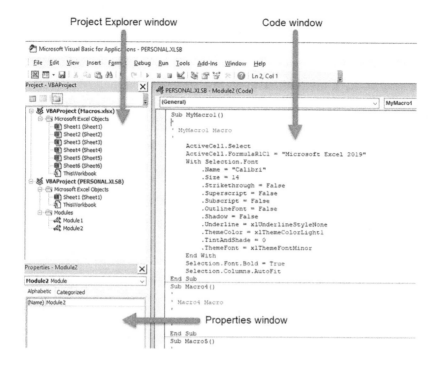

The **Code window** shows the code instructions for the macro. This is where you would edit the macro. The Project Explorer enables you to navigate to macros saved in different modules or in different workbooks that are currently open.

In the **Code window**, the macro code is between a starting keyword and an ending keyword. The beginning of the macro has the keyword **Sub** *MyMacro1()*, where *MyMacro1* is the name you gave to your macro when you created it. The end of the macro is denoted by the keyword **End Sub**. To make changes to the macro, ensure you keep your edits within this area.

The code below was generated from the macro we created earlier in this chapter.

```
Sub MyMacro1 ()
'
' MyMacro1 Macro
'
    ActiveCell.Select
    ActiveCell.FormulaR1C1 = "Microsoft Excel 2019"
    With Selection.Font
        .Name = "Calibri"
        .Size = 14
        .Strikethrough = False
        .Superscript = False
        .Subscript = False
        .OutlineFont = False
        .Shadow = False
        .Underline = xlUnderlineStyleNone
        .ThemeColor = xlThemeColorLight1
        .TintAndShade = 0
        .ThemeFont = xlThemeFontMinor
    End With
    Selection.Font.Bold = True
    Selection.Columns.AutoFit
End Sub
```

After making your changes, save the changes by clicking the **Save** button on the Visual Basic Editor toolbar (the blue disk icon).

To close the Visual Basic Editor, simply click on the **Close** button on the top right of the window (x icon). You can also close the window by clicking on **File > Close and Return to Microsoft Excel**.

Tip: Another way to open the Visual Basic Editor is from the Developer tab on the Ribbon. On the **Developer** tab, in the **Code** group, click the **Visual Basic** command button. The Developer tab is not one of the default tabs on the Excel Ribbon so if you don't have this tab, follow the steps detailed in a previous section of this chapter for how to add the Developer tab to the Excel Ribbon.

7. ANALYZE ALTERNATIVE DATA SETS WITH WHAT-IF ANALYSIS

Spreadsheet formulas are very good at automatically updating results based on your input. For that reason, spreadsheets are one of the best tools for carrying out financial projections based on assumptions. Excel provides a whole raft of tools for just this purpose.

In this chapter, we will be covering:
- What-If Analysis for one-variable and two-variable data tables.
- The Scenario Manager which you can use to create and compare different scenarios for your data.
- The Goal Seek tool to set a goal and allow Excel to adjust other values to meet the goal.
- The Solver add-in tool which can be used to generate scenarios for more complex data.

In Excel, there are different types of what-if analysis you can carry out. In this chapter, we will cover four types that are commonly used in Excel.

- **Data tables**: This feature enables you to generate a series of projections based on one or two changing variables.

- **Goal seeking**: This feature enables you to set a predetermined goal and then choose the variables that will change to meet this goal.

- **Scenarios**: In this type of What-If Analysis, you create different scenarios using alternate figures which you can then compare side-by-side in a generated report.

- **Solver**: The solver is an Excel add-in that you can use to create more complex What-If Analysis, enabling you to use multiple variables and constraints.

7.1 Data Tables

A data table gives you a projection of how your bottom line would look if one or two variables in your data are changed. For example, what would be our profit if we achieved a growth rate in sales of 1.5% rather than 1%? What would be our net profit next year if we reduced our expenses by 3%? These are the kinds of questions that can be answered by a data table.

Creating a One-Variable Data Table

The one-variable data table is a projection based on a series of values that you want to substitute for a single input value.

To demonstrate this type of data table, we will use an example where we create a series of projected sales for the next quarter.

In this example, we have the following figures:
- Sales for quarter one: $45,000.
- Projected growth in sales for quarter two: 2.0%.
- Projected sales for quarter two: 45,000 + (45,000*0.02).

For this projection, we want to substitute different growth rates into the projected growth for Qtr 2 to see a series of projected sales based on different growth rates.

For the column values, we enter rates ranging from 1% to 5% in cells B8:B16, with an increment of 0.5%. You can choose whatever increment you want here.

B5		▼	⋮	✕	✓	*fx*	=B3+(B3*B4)	

◢	A	B	C	D
1	**Projected sales for Quarter 2 - one-variable data table**			
2				
3	Sales Qtr 1	$45,000.00		
4	Growth Qtr 2	2.00%		
5	Projected Sales Qtr 2	$45,900.00		
6				
7			$45,900.00	
8		1.00%		
9		1.50%		
10		2.00%		
11		2.50%		
12		3.00%		
13		3.50%		
14		4.00%		
15		4.50%		
16		5.00%		
17				

For the row value, that is, cell **C7**, we enter =*B5* which is a reference to the master formula which calculates **Projected Sales Qtr 2**. This master formula will be used by the data table as the base figure for which to make the projections.

Once your data has been prepared, as shown above, follow the steps below to generate the data table:

1. Select the table. For this example, it'll be B7:C16.

2. On the Excel Ribbon, click on the **Data** tab, in the **Forecast** group, click on the **What-If Analysis** command button and select **Data Table** from the drop-down menu.

This will display the **Data Table** dialog box. As this is the one-variable data table, we need just one of the fields. Click the **Column input cell** field and then on the worksheet, select the growth percentage, which is cell **B4**.

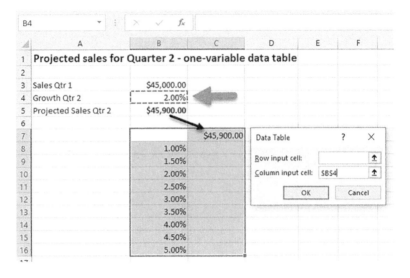

Click **OK** to generate the projected values in cells C8:C16.

	A	B	C	D
			{=TABLE(,B4)}	
1	Projected sales for Quarter 2 - one-variable data table			
2				
3	Sales Qtr 1	$45,000.00		
4	Growth Qtr 2	2.00%		
5	Projected Sales Qtr 2	$45,900.00		
6				
7			$45,900.00	
8		1.00%	$45,450.00	
9		1.50%	$45,675.00	
10		2.00%	$45,900.00	
11		2.50%	$46,125.00	
12		3.00%	$46,350.00	
13		3.50%	$46,575.00	
14		4.00%	$46,800.00	
15		4.50%	$47,025.00	
16		5.00%	$47,250.00	
17				

The data table is created as an array formula using the TABLE function. The TABLE function takes two arguments *row_ref* and/or *column_ref* but only needs one for a one-variable data table.

{=TABLE(,B4)}

The formula shows that the value in cell B4 represents its *column_ref* argument for which alternate values are provided in cells B8:B16. The process simply substitutes the original rate in B4 with the series of rates in B8:B16 to generate the projection.

As the data table uses an array formula, Excel will not allow you to delete only some of the values in the array. To delete values in the data table, you must select all the generated values, that is, cells C8:C16 and hit the **Delete** key.

Creating a Two-Variable Data Table

A two-variable data table enables you to create projections based on the changing values of two variables.

The method of creating a two-variable table is similar to the one-variable data table described above but, in this case, we have two variables that can change instead of one.

A two-variable data table requires input for the column and row fields, so we need a series of values for the first column and first row of the table. At the intersection of the row and column, we enter the master formula which would have the figure that we want to use as the bases of our projection.

To demonstrate this type of data table, we will use an example where we create a series of projected sales for the next quarter based on two variables.

In this example, we have the following figures:
- Sales for quarter one: $45,000.
- Projected growth in sales for quarter two: 2.0%.
- Expenses for quarter two: 15%.
- Projected sales for quarter two: 45,000 + (45,000*0.02).

We want to see a projection for how our sales would look with different growth rates (between 1% and 5%) and different expense rates (between 15% and 30%).

B6			×	✓	f_x	=B3+(B3*B4)-(B3*B5)		

	A	B	C	D	E	F
1	Projection on sales - two-variable data table					
2						
3	Sales Qtr 1	$45,000.00				
4	Growth Qtr 2	1.80%				
5	Expenses Qtr 2	15%				
6	Projected Sales Qtr 2	£39,060.00				
7						
8		£39,060.00	15%	20%	25%	30%
9		1.00%				
10		1.50%				
11		2.00%				
12		2.50%				
13		3.00%				
14		3.50%				
15		4.00%				
16		4.50%				
17		5.00%				

For the row entries, to be substituted with **Expenses Qtr 2**, we enter a series of values ranging from 15% to 30% in cells C8:F8.

For the column entries, to be substituted with **Growth Qtr 2**, we enter a series of values ranging from 1% to 5% (increasing by 0.5%) in cells B9:B17.

In cell B8 we enter =B6 which is a reference to the master formula that calculates **Projected Sales Qtr 2**.

Once your worksheet model has been prepared as shown in the image above, follow the steps below to generate the data table:

1. Select the table. For this example, it'll be B8:F17.

2. On the Excel Ribbon, click on the **Data** tab, in the **Forecast** group, click on the **What-If Analysis** command button and select **Data Table** from the drop-down menu.

    This will display the **Data Table** dialog box. As this is a two-variable data table, we need to enter both fields in the Data Table dialog box.

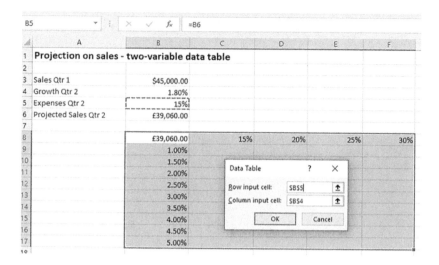

3. Click inside the **Row input cell** field and then on the worksheet, select the expenses for quarter two, which is cell **B5**.

4. Next, click in the **Column input cell** field and then on the worksheet, select the growth percentage, which is cell **B4**.

5. Click **OK** to generate the projected values in the data table.

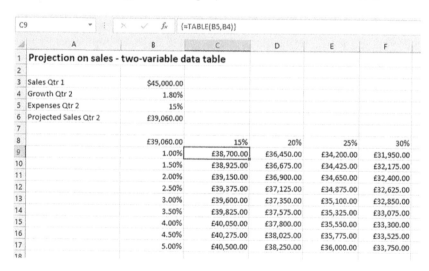

The two-variable data table uses the TABLE function to create an array formula in the output range of C9:F17. The TABLE function takes two arguments *row_ref* and/or *column_ref*.

{=TABLE(B5,B4)}

The formula shows that cell B5 is the *row_ref* argument for which alternate values have been provided in cells B9:B17. The *column_ref* argument has cell B4 for which we have alternate values in cells C8:F8.

The process simply substitutes the original values with the series of values created in B9:B17 and C8:F8 to generate the projection.

As the data table uses an array formula, you can't delete only some of the values in the array. To delete the generated data in the table, you must select all values in cells C9:F17 and hit the **Delete** key.

7.2 Scenario Manager

Another tool provided by Excel that you can use to create a What-If Analysis is the Scenario Manager. The Scenario Manager enables you to create different scenarios where certain input values are changed to produce different results.

You can assign names the different scenarios in the scenario manager, for example, *Most Likely*, *Best Case*, and *Worst Case*. Once you've created the scenarios in the Scenario Manager, you can view the different scenario in your worksheet or generate a summary report with all the scenarios so that you can compare them side-by-side.

In the following example, we will create several projections for the next year based on figures from the current year. The scenarios will apply different growth rates to the current figures so that we can compare the scenarios together in a summary report.

Figures – Current Year
- Sales: $627,198.00
- Cost of production: $200,000
- Office supplies: $5,000
- Vehicle: $10,500.00
- Building: $50,000.00

C4		f_x	=B4+(B4*D4)	
	A	B	C	D
1	**Projection Scenarios**			
2				
3		Current	Projected	Growth assumptions
4	Sales	$627,198.00	$639,741.96	2.00%
5	Cost of production	($200,000.00)	($203,000.00)	1.50%
6	Office supplies	($5,000.00)	($5,075.00)	1.50%
7	Vehicle	($10,500.00)	($10,657.50)	1.50%
8	Building	($50,000.00)	($50,750.00)	1.50%
9	Profit	$361,698.00	$370,259.46	
10				

The projected value in C4 is calculated with the following formula:

=B4+(B4*D4)

The formula in **Projected** simply increments the **Current** value by the percentage rate in **Growth assumption**. The same formula is used to derive the values in cells C5:C8.

We want to create more scenarios using different growth assumptions without overwriting the original data as we want to be able to compare multiple scenarios together. This is where the Scenario Manager comes in.

Tip: When using the Scenario Manager, it is a good idea to name each cell you intend to change. It makes it easier to know what each cell represents when you enter the new values in a subsequent dialog box. It also makes any subsequent reports you create of the scenarios easier to understand. Named Ranges are covered in my *Excel 2019 Basics* book.

Follow the steps below to create different scenarios with the Scenario Manager:

1. Select the changing cells in the worksheet. In this case, the changing cells are D4:D8.

2. On the **Data** tab, in the **Forecast** group, click **What-If Analysis** command button and select **Scenario Manager** from the drop-down menu.

    The **Scenario Manager** dialog box will be opened.

3. Click on the **Add** button to add a new scenario.

4. Enter a name for the scenario in the **Scenario name** field. These can be names like *Most likely, Best case, Worst case* etc.

5. The **Changing cells** field should already have the reference to the cells you selected before opening the Scenario Manager dialog box. However, if the right cells have not been selected, click on the Expand Dialog box button on the field (up arrow) and select the cells in the worksheet.

6. The **Comment** box is optional. You can enter a short description for the scenario or leave the default text which is a log of when it was last updated.

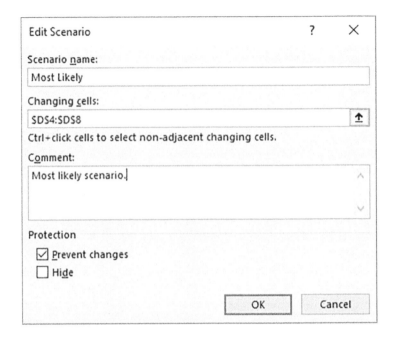

7. In the **Protection** portion of the screen, leave the **Prevent changes** checkbox selected if you want Excel to protect the scenario from changes when worksheet protection is turned on. If you don't want to protect the scenario when the worksheet is protected, uncheck Prevent changes.

8. If you don't want the scenario hidden when worksheet protection is on, leave the **Hide** check box unselected. Alternatively, if you want Excel to hide the scenario when the worksheet is protected, select the Hide check box.

   Note: Worksheet protection is a separate topic that's not related to What-If Analysis and covered elsewhere in this book.

9. Click **OK** to open the **Scenario Values** dialog box.

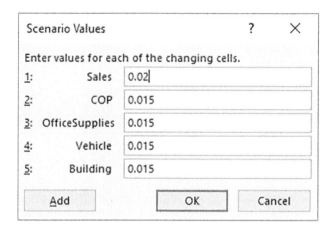

10. The Scenario Values dialog box contains several fields for the changing cells. As you can see from the image above, naming the changing cells becomes useful here as each field is labelled with a name rather than a cell reference.

    For the first scenario, you may want to accept the values already in the fields (if you had values in the cells before starting the Scenario Manager). If you want a different set of values for your first scenario, you can change them here.

11. When done, click the **Add** button to save the scenario and go back to the **Add Scenario** dialog box.

12. Repeat steps **4** to **11** above to add the other scenarios you want to create.

After you finish creating the different scenarios you want to add, you can close the Scenario Values dialog box and then return to the Scenario Manager dialog box. Now, in the Scenario Manager dialog box, you'll see the names of all the scenarios you've added in the **Scenarios** list box.

To show the scenario that you have entered, select the scenario in the **Scenarios** list box and click on the **Show** command button. You can also just double-click on the name of the scenario in the list box to show the scenario in the worksheet. For example, to display the *Best Case* scenario, double-click on *Best Case*. This will close the Scenario Manager dialog box and insert the rates we entered for the *Best Case* scenario in our table.

To delete a scenario, select it in the list box and click on the **Delete** button. This will remove that scenario from the scenario manager.

To edit a scenario, select the scenario in the **Scenarios** list box and click on the **Edit** button. This will take you through the editing process where you can change the name of the scenario, the changing cells, and the values for the cells. If you only want to change just the values, then click through until you get to the **Scenario Values** dialog box and change the values there.

The Scenario Manager dialog box also enables you to merge scenarios from other Excel workbooks that are open. Note that the workbooks must share the same data layout and changing cells for you to be able to merge their scenarios.

To merge scenarios from another workbook, do the following:

1. Click the **Merge** button in the Scenario Manager dialog box. This will display the **Merge Scenarios** dialog box.

2. Select the workbook name from the **Book** drop-down list box.

3. In the **Sheet** list box, select the worksheet and then click **OK**.

All the scenarios in that worksheet are then copied and merged with the current worksheet.

Summary Reports

After creating the different scenarios, you can compare them side-by-side in a summary report.

To generate a summary report for the scenarios you have entered:

1. In the Scenario Manager dialog box, click on the **Summary** button. This will open the **Scenario Summary** dialog box.

2. Select **Report type** if it is not already selected.

3. Click the **Results cells** text box and select the result cells in your worksheet. These would be the cells with the totals for your projection. For our example, our **Profit** cell is C9.

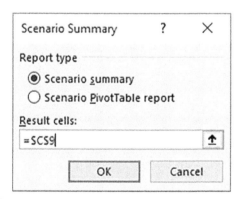

4. Click on **OK** to generate the report.

Excel will generate a report in a separate worksheet showing you all the scenarios you have created.

Scenario Summary				
	Current Values:	Most Likely	Best Case	Worst Case
Changing Cells:				
Sales	2.00%	2.00%	5.00%	1.00%
COP	1.50%	1.50%	1.00%	8.00%
OfficeSupplies	1.50%	1.50%	1.00%	2.50%
Vehicle	1.50%	1.50%	1.00%	5.00%
Building	1.50%	1.50%	1.20%	5.00%
Result Cells:				
Profit	$370,259.46	$370,259.46	$390,302.90	$348,819.98

Notes: Current Values column represents values of changing cells at time Scenario Summary Report was created. Changing cells for each scenario are highlighted in gray.

As you can see from the image above, assigning names to the changing cells and result cells in your worksheet comes in handy when producing a scenario summary.

Now, you may wonder why we need to use the scenario manager when we could have just entered the different scenarios directly in the Excel worksheet area. The example used here with the scenario manager is simple for demonstration purposes only. However, the scenario manager comes in handy when the complexity of the data model would make it difficult to enter the different scenarios side-by-side in Excel in a meaningful way.

7.3 Goal Seeking

On some occasions, when working with data in Excel, you already have the outcome that you want to achieve in mind, and you would like to know the various input values that will achieve that outcome or goal. For example, you may have a goal of $600,000 in revenue and to achieve that goal you need a certain amount for your sales against the cost of expenses. This is where the Goal Seek feature in Excel comes in.

The Goal Seek command in Excel enables you to set a goal in one cell and then choose the cell whose value you would like Excel to adjust in other to meet your goal. So, this is like working backwards, stating the results first and allowing Goal Seek to determine the inputs needed to meet that goal. The goal cell will have a formula which is based on the input from other cells, including the cell that Excel will be changing.

For example, let's say we want to find how much sales we need to generate to reach a certain level of income. Instead of making several adjustments to the sales figure in trying to produce the desired result, we can simply set the result we want and let Goal Seek work out the sales figure required to achieve the result.

To demonstrate the goal seeking feature in Excel, we'll use an example to forecast the income based on a range of input values.

B8		✕ ✓ f_x	=B6+B7
	A	B	C
1	**Income Forecast for 2020**		
2			
3			
4	Sales	$600,250.00	
5	Cost of production	($139,705.00)	
6	Gross Profit	$460,545.00	
7	Expenses	($84,267.00)	
8	Income	$376,278.00	
9			

In the table above, cell **B8** has a formula that calculates the *Income*, which is the sum of the *Gross Profit* and the *Expenses* (this is a negative value as denoted by brackets).

=B6+B7

Our goal seeking question is, what amount should our sales be if we want to generate an income of $500,000?

Once the data structure has been created in the worksheet, follow the steps below to get to perform the goal seeking:

1. On the Excel Ribbon, click the **Data** tab, then In the **Forecast** group, click the **What-If Analysis** command button and select **Goal Seek** from the drop-down menu. This will display the **Goal Seek** dialog box.

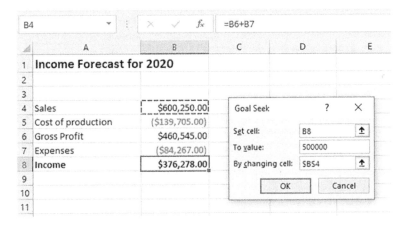

2. Click in the **Set cell** text box and select the cell in the worksheet that contains the formula that will return the value you're seeking. For our example, this is cell **B8**.

3. In the **To value** text box, enter the value that you want to set the cell to. For our example, the value will be 500,000.

4. Click in the **By changing cell** text box and select the cell that contains the value you want Excel to adjust to achieve the goal. For this example, this will be cell **B4**.

5. Click **OK** when done.

Excel will display the **Goal Seek Status** dialog box which informs you that a solution has been found and that the result value is now the same as the target value.

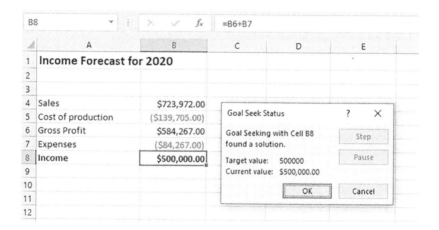

If the Goal Seek does not find a solution it will enable the **Step** and **Pause** buttons to enable you to step through different options to find a solution.

6. If you want to keep the solution found as a result of the goal seeking process, click **OK** to dismiss the Goal Seek Status dialog box. If you don't want to keep the result, simply click the **Cancel** button.

Note that if you accept the value by clicking OK, it will overwrite your existing values. You can switch back to the old the value by clicking the **Undo** button on the Quick Access Toolbar or by using the Ctrl+Z keystroke.

To switch back and forth between the previous value and the value returned by Goal Seek, you can use the **Undo** and **Redo** buttons on the Quick Access Toolbar. Alternatively, you can press Ctrl+Z to display the original values and Ctrl+Y to display the solution returned by the goal seeking command.

7.4 The Solver Add-in

The Data Table and Goal Seek commands are great for creating What-If Analysis solutions for simpler problems that require a direct relationship between the inputs and the outputs. However, for more complex problems, Excel provides another tool, which is the **Solver** add-in utility.

The Solver can be used when you need to create a solution that requires changing multiple input values in your model. The Solver also enables you to impose constraints on the input and output values.

The Solver uses an iterative method to find the optimum solution based on the inputs, the desired result, and the constraints you have set.

Complex problems can have different ways that they're solved and what the Solver does is try to present the best solution for you. However, this may not necessarily be the best one for your particular case. For example, if several variables need to be changed, the Solver may produce a combination of figures that may not suit your specific needs (even if the result meets the objective). This is why you may want to run the Solver multiple times to get the best solution for you.

To set up the problem in the Solver, you will need to define the following items:

- **Objective cell**: This is the target cell that is set to maximum, minimum, or a specific value. The objective cell needs to be a formula.

- **Variable cells**: These are the changing cells in your worksheet. The Goal Seek method, for example, enables you to only specify one cell that can be changed. The difference with the Solver is that you can have multiple cells that can be changed to achieve the objective.

- **Constraints**: These are the cells that contain the values you want to use to set a limit or restriction to the range of changes that can be made. For example, you could set a constraint that says the *Sales* figure cannot be increased by more than 10% to achieve the solution (perhaps because a sales figure of more than 10% would be unrealistic for this particular problem).

After setting the parameters in the Solver, Excel returns the optimum solution by changing the values in your worksheet. At this point, you have the option of retaining the changes in your worksheet or restoring your original values. The Solver also enables you to save the solution as a scenario which you can view at a later time.

The Solver can be used with the Scenario Manager to set up a problem to solve. The variable cells that you define when you use the Scenario Manager to set up a scenario are available and picked up by the Solver. The Solver also allows you to save solutions as scenarios which will then be available to the Scenario Manager.

Adding the Solver Add-in utility to the Excel Ribbon

The Solver is an add-in and may not be available on your Ribbon if it hasn't been manually added as it is not added by default when you install Excel 2019.

Follow the steps below to add the Solver command button to your Excel Ribbon:

1. Click on **File > Options > Add-ins**.

2. At the bottom of the Add-ins tab, ensure that the **Manage** drop-down list has **Excel Add-ins** selected.

3. Click on **Go** to show the **Add-ins** dialog box. In the Add-ins dialog box, check the **Solver Add-in** check box and click on the **OK** button.

The **Solver** command button can be found on the **Data** tab, in the **Analyze** group.

In the following example, we will be using the Solver to find a solution to what combination of figures can generate an income of $680,500.00. The worksheet model created for the problem is shown below.

| C4 | | | ✗ | ✓ | *fx* | =$B$4+($B$4*SalesGrowth) |

	A	B	C	D
1	**Sales Forecast**			
2				
3		Qtr 1	Qtr 2	Assumptions
4	Sales	$800,250.40	$840,262.92	5%
5	Cost of production	($139,705.00)	($148,087.30)	6%
6	Gross Profit	$660,545.40	$692,175.62	
7	Expenses	($84,267.00)	($90,165.69)	7%
8	Income	$576,278.40	$602,009.93	
9				

The value in C4 is calculated with the following formula:

=$B$4+($B$4*SalesGrowth)

SalesGrowth is the name given to cell **D4** which is currently 5%. The formulas in the **Qtr 2** column simply increments the **Qtr 1** values by the growth rates under **Assumptions**.

For this example, the changing/variable cells will be those in the Assumptions column while the result/objective cell will be **C8** (which is named **Income_Qtr2**).

Once you have loaded the Solver add-in and created your worksheet model, follow the steps below to define a problem with the Solver:

1. On the **Data** tab, in the **Analyze** group, click the **Solver** command button. Excel opens the **Solver Parameters** dialog box.

2. In the **Solver Parameters** dialog box, the **Set Objective** textbox is the result you want to achieve. This needs to be a cell in the worksheet with a formula. Click the text box and then select the cell on your worksheet. For our example, this is cell **C8** on the worksheet. The name of the cell is **Income_Qtr2** so the name is inserted in the text box.

3. You have the option of setting the objective to a maximum (as large as possible based on the input values available), a minimum (as small as possible), or to a specific value. For this example, we are using a specific value for our objective, so, click **Value Of** and enter 680500.

4. Click the **By Changing Variable Cells** text box and select the cells you want to change in the worksheet. To select non-adjacent cells, simply hold down the **Ctrl** key while clicking on the cells. If you have given the variable cells names, the names will be entered in place of the cell references.

5. In the **Subject to the Constraints** list box, you can add constraints to place restrictions on the extent of changes the Solver can make. To add a constraint, click the **Add** button. This will display the **Add Constraint** dialog box.

6. Click the **Cell Reference** text box, then select the cell in the worksheet for which you want to create a constraint.

Select the relationship from the drop-down list box in the middle. The options are: =, <=, >=, int (for integer), and bin (for binary). For our example, we select <= from the drop-down list.

In the **Constraint** text box, enter the constraint. For our example, we don't want the *SalesGrowth* to be more than 15% so we enter 15%.

Click **Add** to insert the constraint and continue adding more constraints (or click **OK** to return to the Solver Parameters dialog box if you're done).

The constraint you added will now be listed in the **Subject to the Constraints** list box.

7. For our example, we'll leave the **Make Unconstrained Variables Non-Negative** checkbox selected, which is the default. Deselect this checkbox if you want to allow negative values in variable cells for which you've set no constraints.

8. The default value for the **Select a Solving Method** drop-down list will have the default value is **GRG Nonlinear**.

There are three solving methods:
- **GRG Nonlinear** is for solving smooth nonlinear problems.
- **Simplex LP** method is for linear problems.
- **Evolutionary** method is for non-smooth problems.

Leave this selection as the default - GRG Nonlinear, unless you're sure one of the other methods is more optimal for your problem.

There is a brief description of the solving methods in the label below the drop-down list box.

9. Once you've entered all the parameters in the Solver Parameters dialog box, click **Solve** button.

Solver Results

When you click Solve on the Solver Parameters dialog box, the box will disappear and depending on how complex your problem is, you may see an indicator on Excel's status bar informing you of the progress of the Solver. On most occasions, however, the solution would be generated quickly, and the **Solver Results** dialog box will be displayed.

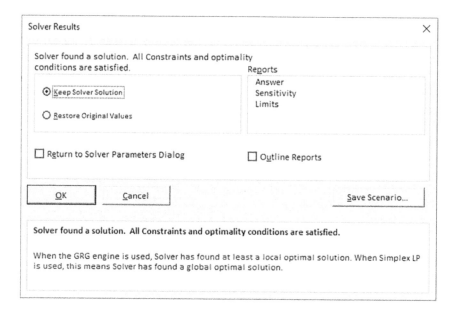

The **Solver Results** dialog box informs you whether a solution was found for your problem or not. If a solution were not found, the dialog box will inform you that a solution could not be found, and you will have the opportunity to go back and adjust the parameters.

If a solution was found, the Solver will display the new values in your worksheet, but the Solver Results dialog box will give you the option to keep the values provided by the solution or restore your original values.

To keep the solution found by the Solver, select **Keep Solver Solution** (if it is not already selected), then click **OK**.

	A	B	C	D	E
1	Sales Forecast				
2					
3		Qtr 1	Qtr 2	Assumptions	
4	Sales	$800,250.40	$915,620.72	14%	
5	Cost of production	($139,705.00)	($145,790.62)	4%	
6	Gross Profit	$660,545.40	$769,830.10		
7	Expenses	($84,267.00)	($89,330.10)	6%	
8	Income	$576,278.40	$680,500.00		
9					
10					
11					
12					

From the worksheet model in the image above, you can see that the Solver changed the growth percentages for *Sales* (14%), *Cost of Production* (4%), and *Expenses* (6%), to achieve the target *Income* for *Qtr 2* of £680,500.00. You may also notice that the Solver stayed within the 15% constraint set for the *SalesGrowth* cell.

If you do not want to keep the solution and instead return to the original values in your worksheet, select the **Restore Original Values** option.

To save the solution as a scenario before restoring your original values, click the **Save Scenario** button and assign a name to it. Once you have saved it, you can then select the Restore Original Values option and click **OK** to close the Solver Results dialog box.

You can also click the **Cancel** button on the Solver Results dialog box to dismiss the Solver and return your original values.

Note: If you choose to keep the solution provided by the Solver, unlike the Goal Seek command, you can't undo the changes by clicking the Undo command on the Quick Access Toolbar. If you want to retain your original values, select **Restore Original Values,** and then click on **Save Scenario** to save the scenario for later viewing. That way, you can keep your original values in the worksheet and use the Scenario Manager (covered previously in this chapter) to display the solution generated by the Solver.

Solver Options

The default options used by the Solver is adequate for most problems, however, in some situations, you may want to change the options before generating a solution with the Solver.

To change the Solver options, click the **Options** button in the Solver Parameters dialog box. Excel opens the **Options** dialog box which has three tabs: All Methods, GRG Nonlinear, and Evolutionary.

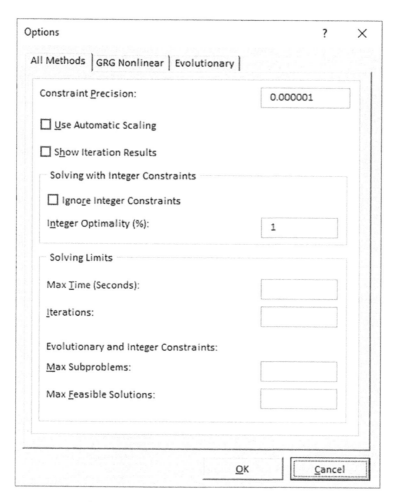

The following settings apply to the Solver options.

- **Constraint precision**: This specifies the precision of the constraints added. To satisfy a constraint, the relationship between the cell reference and the value of the constraint cannot be more than this amount. The smaller this number is, the higher the precision.

- **Use automatic scaling**: Select this option if you want the Solver to automatically scale the results.

- **Show iteration results**: Select this option if you want the Solver to show the results for the iterations it followed in solving the problem.

- **Ignore integer constraints**: Select this checkbox if you want the Solver to ignore any constraints that you specified that use integers.

- **Integer optimality (%)**: This option specifies the percentage of integer optimality that the Solver applies when solving the problem.

- **Max time (Seconds)**: This value specifies the maximum number of seconds that you want the Solver to spend in finding a solution before it times out.

- **Iterations**: This value specifies the maximum number of iterations you want the Solver to make in recalculating the worksheet when finding the solution.

- **Max Subproblems**: This value specifies the maximum number of subproblems that you want the Solver to take when using the Evolutionary method in solving the problem.

- **Max feasible solutions**: This value specifies the maximum number of feasible solutions that you want the Solver to pursue when using the Evolutionary method in solving the problem.

Note that the Options dialog box also has the **GRG Nonlinear** and **Evolutionary** tabs where you can make additional changes to the settings.

After making changes to the Solver options, click **OK** to return to the Solver Parameters dialog box.

Tip: Only make a change to an option in the Solver if you understand what that setting represents and how the change will affect your worksheet model, otherwise the default values will suffice for most Solver problems.

Saving and Loading Solver Problem Models

When you save your workbook, the objective cell, variable cells, constraint, and Solver options that were last entered in the Solver Parameters dialog box are saved as part of the worksheet. These parameters will be loaded in the Solver Parameters dialog box the next time it is opened.

When you create other problem models for the worksheet that you want to also save, you must use the **Load/Save** button in the Solver Parameters dialog box to save them.

When you click the **Load/Save** button, Excel displays the **Load/Save Model** dialog box.

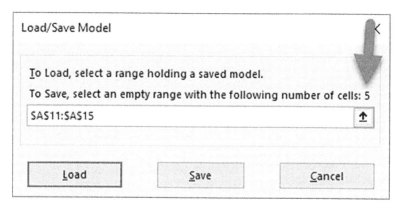

To **Save**, click the text box in the Load/Save Model dialog box and select an empty vertical range in your worksheet with enough cells to hold all the parameters you entered for the problem model. To help, the message in the Load/Save Model dialog box will tell you how many cells you need to select.

Once you have entered the range in the text box, click the **Save** button and the values will be saved to that range in your worksheet.

To **Load** a saved model, click the text box, and then select the range in your worksheet with the saved model, then click the **Load** button. The parameters saved in the range will then be loaded in the Solver Parameters dialog box.

Solver Reports

There are three types of reports you can create from the Solver Results dialog box:

- **Answer**: This report lists the result cell and the variable cells with their original values, final values, and any constraints used as parameters.

- **Sensitivity**: This report shows you how sensitive an optimal solution is to changes in the formulas behind the objective cell and constraints.

- **Limits**: This report displays the objective cell and the variable cells with their values, lower and upper limits, and results. The lower limit is the lowest value that the variable cells can have while still meeting the constraints. The upper limit represents the highest value that will do this.

To generate a report, in the Solver Results dialog box, select one or more of the reports in the **Reports** list box before clicking **OK**.

You can generate one or all of the reports as the Reports list box allows you to select more than one item on the list. When you click **OK**, Excel will generate the selected reports in separate worksheets, adding them to the beginning of the workbook.

8. ANALYZE DATA DYNAMICALLY WITH PIVOTTABLES AND PIVOTCHARTS

There are different ways you can create pivot tables in Excel 2019. We will focus here on the different methods you can use to create pivot tables, including how to generate pivot charts from the pivoted data.

In this chapter, we will cover:

- How to create pivot tables with the Quick Analysis tool.
- How to create a Recommended PivotTable.
- How to create a pivot table manually.
- How to filter, sort and format pivot tables.
- How to create a pivot chart.

An Excel PivotTable is a powerful tool that enables you to dynamically calculate, summarise, and analyze data from different perspectives.

There are several methods for creating a new pivot table in Excel 2019:

- **Quick Analysis tool**: This option auto-generates a pivot table for you. When you select all the cells in your data list and click the Quick Analysis tool on the Tables tab, you get a list of pre-designed pivot tables for your data from which you can choose. When you select one, Excel inserts the pivot table in a new worksheet.

- **Recommended PivotTables button**: This option auto-generates a pivot table for you. When you select one cell in your data list and click on the Recommended PivotTables button on the Insert tab, you get a list of recommended pivot tables from which you can choose. When you select one, Excel inserts the pivot table in a new worksheet.

- **PivotTable button**: This option enables you to create a pivot table manually. When you select one cell in your data list and click on the PivotTable button on the Insert tab, Excel opens the Create PivotTable dialog box where you specify your data source and location of the pivot table before manually selecting the fields to use from the data.

8.1 Preparing Your Data

Some preparation is required to get a data list ready for a pivot table. The source data used for a pivot table needs to be organised as a list or converted to an Excel table (this is recommended although not compulsory).

A few steps to prepare the source data for a pivot table:

1. The data should have column headings in a single row on top.

2. Remove any temporary totals or summaries that are not part of the core data.

3. The data cannot have empty rows, so, delete any empty rows.

4. Ensure you do not have any extraneous data surrounding the list.

5. You may also want to convert the range to an Excel table (although it is not compulsory).

	A	B	C	D	E	F	G	H
1	Employee	Product	Customer	Order Date	Ship City	Item Cost	No. of Items	Total Cost
2	Anne Hellung-Larsen	Cora Fabric Chair	Acme LTD	11/24/2016	Las Vegas	$475.00	20	$9,500.00
3	Jan Kotas	Lukah Leather Chair	Elgin Homes	05/13/2016	New York	$345.00	9	$3,105.00
4	Mariya Sergienko	Habitat Oken Console Table	Mecury Builders	04/28/2016	Las Vegas	$36.00	28	$1,008.00
5	Michael Neipper	Hygena Fabric Chair	Infinity Homes	11/06/2016	Portland	$407.00	23	$9,361.00
6	Anne Hellung-Larsen	Harley Fabric Cuddle Chair	Elgin Homes	07/16/2016	New York	$803.00	20	$16,060.00
7	Jan Kotas	Windsor 2 Seater Cuddle Chair	B&B Seaside	04/27/2017	Denver	$302.00	8	$2,416.00
8	Mariya Sergienko	Fabric Chair	B&B Seaside	06/26/2016	Los Angelas	$425.00	11	$4,675.00
9	Laura Giussani	Verona 1 Shelf Telephone Table	Home Designers	04/07/2016	Milwaukee	$282.00	8	$2,256.00
10	Anne Hellung-Larsen	Floral Fabric Tub Chair	Acorn USA	08/17/2016	Memphis	$158.00	2	$316.00
11	Jan Kotas	Fabric Chair in a Box	Infinity Homes	04/20/2017	Portland	$857.00	28	$23,996.00
12	Mariya Sergienko	Slimline Console Table	Apex Homes	11/01/2016	Chicago	$534.00	29	$15,486.00
13	Nancy Freehafer	Collection Martha Fabric Wingback Chair	Empire Homes	09/24/2017	Boise	$137.00	15	$2,055.00
14	Nancy Freehafer	Slimline Console Table	Apex Homes	04/15/2017	Chicago	$433.00	16	$6,928.00
15	Nancy Freehafer	Fabric Wingback Chair	Express Builders	09/03/2016	Miami	$210.00	2	$420.00
16	Nancy Freehafer	Fabric Chair in a Box - Denim Blue	Impressive Homes	04/23/2016	Seattle	$634.00	14	$8,876.00
17	Nancy Freehafer	Tessa Fabric Chair	Acorn USA	02/10/2017	Memphis	$252.00	23	$5,796.00
18	Robert Zare	Collection Bradley Riser Recline Fabric Chair	Northern Contractors	01/05/2016	Salt Lake City	$281.00	5	$1,405.00
19	Michael Neipper	Fabric Wingback Chair	Home Designers	05/15/2017	Milwaukee	$405.00	30	$12,150.00
20	Mariya Sergienko	Tessa Fabric Chair	Infinity Homes	05/11/2017	Portland	$472.00	5	$2,360.00

Once the data has been prepared, you can now create a pivot table.

8.2 Create a PivotTable with the Quick Analysis Tool

In Excel 2019, you can quickly create a pivot table for your data list by using the Quick Analysis tool. If you're not that familiar with creating pivot tables but you have an idea of want you want to summarize, the Quick Analysis tool will recommend a series of pre-designed options from which you can choose.

Follow the steps below to create a pivot table from the Quick Analysis tool:

1. Select all the data in your data list (including the headings). Note that if you have assigned a range name to your data list, you can select the whole list by choosing the name from the Name box drop-down menu.

2. After you select the data list, the Quick Analysis tool appears on the lower-right of the selection. Click on the **Quick Analysis** tool to open the Quick Analysis palette.

3. Click on the **Tables** tab to display various PivotTable options for your data (after the Table button).

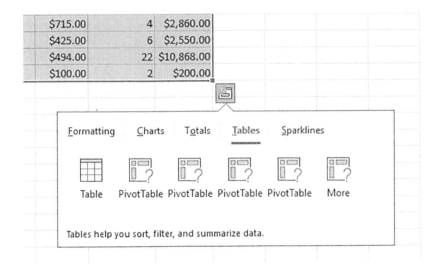

4. To see a live preview of each PivotTable option, move your mouse pointer over each button. You'll see a live preview (i.e. based on your data) of the type of pivot table that option will generate.

5. When you find a preview that you want, click on its button. Excel 2019 then generates the PivotTable in a new worksheet (inserted in front of the worksheet with the source data). You can rename and move this worksheet to a different part of your workbook if you want.

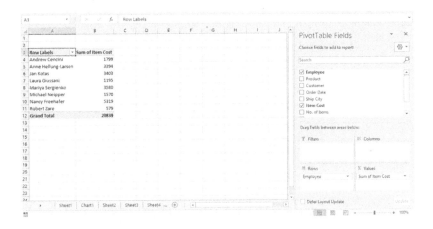

Notes:

- When you select any area in the new pivot table that has been created, the **PivotTable Fields** task pane will be displayed on the right side of the worksheet window. Also, when you click any cell within the pivot table, a **PivotTable Analyze** context tab will be displayed on the ribbon. This context tab provides several tools and commands that you can use to modify and format your pivot table, just as you would if you had created it manually.

- On some occasions, Excel may not be able to suggest pivot table options with the Data Analysis tool, particularly if it can't analyze your data due to how your worksheet model is structured.

When this happens, on the Tables tab of the Quick Analysis palette, a single blank PivotTable button will be displayed after the Table button. You can click that button to manually create your pivot table. We will cover how to manually create pivot tables later in this chapter.

8.3 Create a Recommended PivotTable

Another way to create a pivot table is by using the **Recommended PivotTables** command on the ribbon. This method is even faster than using the Quick Analysis tool (as long as you have prepared the data list with column headings as described earlier in this chapter).

Follow the steps below to use this method to create a pivot table:

1. Click anywhere within the data list for which you want to create a new pivot table.

2. On the **Insert** tab, in the **Tables** group, click on the **Recommended PivotTables** command button.

    Excel will open the **Recommended PivotTables** dialog box which presents a list of pivot table options for your data. You can click on each item on the list to see a live preview on the right pane of the dialog box.

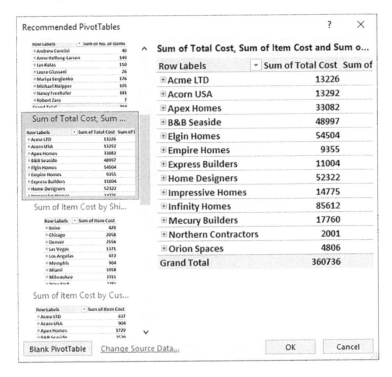

3. Once you find one that has the type of summary you want to create, select the item, and click the **OK** button.

A new pivot table will be created in a new worksheet in front of the worksheet with the data source. With the pivot table selected, the **PivotTable Fields** task pane is displayed on the right side of the worksheet, and the **PivotTable Analyze** contextual tab will be available on the Ribbon.

Note: If none of the options provided meets what you want, click on the **Blank PivotTable** button on the **Recommended PivotTables** dialog box to create the pivot table manually.

8.4 Creating a PivotTable Manually

To create a pivot table:

1. Click on any cell in your range or table.

2. On the **Insert** tab, click the **PivotTable** button.

The **Create PivotTable** dialog box will be displayed.

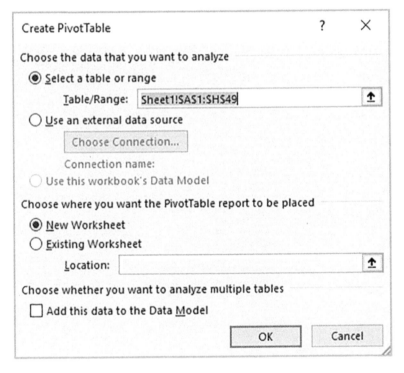

Excel will figure out the table or range you intend to use for your pivot table, and it will select it in the **Table/Range** field. If this is not accurate then you can manually select the range by clicking on the Expand Dialog box button (up arrow) on the field.

The next option on the screen is where you want to place the pivot table. The default location is in a new worksheet. It is best to have your pivot table on a worksheet separate from your source data, so select the **New Worksheet** option here if it's not already selected.

3. Click on **OK**.

A new worksheet will now be created with a PivotTable placeholder, and on the right side, you'll see a dialog box - **PivotTable Fields**.

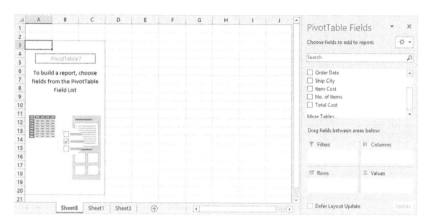

The PivotTable tool has four areas where you can place fields:

Rows, Columns, Values, and **Filters**.

To add a field to your PivotTable, select the checkbox next to the field name in the PivotTable Fields pane. When you select fields, they are added to their default areas. Non-numeric fields are added to the **Rows** box. Date and time fields are added to the **Columns** box. Numeric fields are added to the **Values** box.

You can also drag fields from the list to one of the four areas you want to place it. To move one field to another, you can drag it there.

To remove a field from a box, click on it and click **Remove Field** from the pop-up menu. You can also just uncheck it in the fields list or drag it away from the box and drop it back on the fields list.

Example

In this example, let's say we want a summary of our data that shows the total spent by each Customer.

1. Select the **Customer** field on the list and it will be added to the Rows box. The PivotTable will also be updated with the list of customers as row headings.

2. Next, select the **Total Cost** field and this will be added to the **Values** box.

The PivotTable will now be updated with the **Sum of Total Cost** for each Customer.

Row Labels	Sum of Total Cost
Acme LTD	13226
Acorn USA	13292
Apex Homes	33082
B&B Seaside	48997
Elgin Homes	54504
Empire Homes	9355
Express Builders	11004
Home Designers	52322
Impressive Homes	14775
Infinity Homes	85612
Mecury Builders	17760
Northern Contractors	2001
Orion Spaces	4806
Grand Total	**360736**

So, as you can see, we have been able to get a quick summary of our data with just a few clicks. If we had hundreds of thousands of records, this could have taken many hours to accomplish, if done manually.

We can add more values to the table by dragging them to the Values box from the list.

For example, if we wanted to add the total number of items per customer, we'll select **No. of Items** on the list or drag it to the **Values** box.

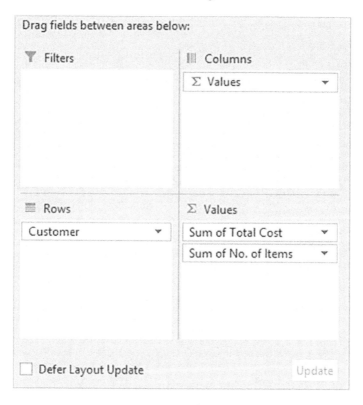

This will add the **Sum of No. of Items** for each customer to the PivotTable as shown in the image below.

Row Labels ▼	Sum of No. of Items	Sum of Total Cost
Acme LTD	43	13226
Acorn USA	53	13292
Apex Homes	73	33082
B&B Seaside	88	48997
Elgin Homes	123	54504
Empire Homes	40	9355
Express Builders	14	11004
Home Designers	94	52322
Impressive Homes	31	14775
Infinity Homes	143	85612
Mecury Builders	52	17760
Northern Contractors	7	2001
Orion Spaces	33	4806
Grand Total	**794**	**360736**

To view the summary from the perspective of **Products**, i.e. the total number of items sold and the total cost for each product, we would put **Product** in the Rows box and both **Total Cost** and **No. of Items** in the Values box.

To view the summary from the perspective of **Employees**, we would place **Employee** in the Rows box, and **No. of Items** and **Total Cost** in the Values box.

Here we see the data summarised by Employee i.e. how many items each employee sold, and the revenue generated.

Row Labels	Sum of No. of Items	Sum of Total Cost
Andrew Cencini	40	21418
Anne Hellung-Larsen	149	53969
Jan Kotas	110	70865
Laura Giussani	26	18690
Mariya Sergienko	176	78334
Michael Neipper	105	40203
Nancy Freehafer	181	75256
Robert Zare	7	2001
Grand Total	**794**	**360736**

If we want to see the number of items sold per city, we will place **Ship City** in the Rows box and **No. of Items** in the Values box.

	Row Labels	Sum of No. of Items
3		
4	Boise	40
5	Chicago	106
6	Denver	45
7	Las Vegas	95
8	Los Angelas	43
9	Memphis	53
10	Miami	44
11	Milwaukee	94
12	New York	93
13	Portland	143
14	Salt Lake City	7
15	Seattle	31
16	**Grand Total**	**794**

8.5 Summarising Data by Date

To display the columns split into years, drag a date field into the Columns box, for example, Order Date. The PivotTable tool will automatically generate PivotTable fields for Quarters and Years. Once these fields have been generated, you should remove the Order Date field from the Columns box and place in the Quarter or Year field, depending on which one you want to use for your summary.

To display the row headings by date, place **Order Date** (or your date field) in the Rows box.

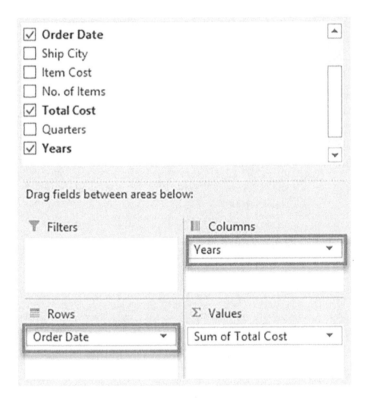

This will produce the following results.

Sum of Total Cost	Column Labels ▾		
Row Labels ▾↓	2016	2017	Grand Total
Jan	39569	7772	47341
Feb		22819	22819
Mar	5502	1854	7356
Apr	22724	57618	80342
May	3105	14510	17615
Jun	24021	596	24617
Jul	16060		16060
Aug	316	12141	12457
Sep	42763	9615	52378
Oct	16752		16752
Nov	34347	9756	44103
Dec	18896		18896
Grand Total	224055	136681	360736

8.6 Applying Formatting

As you can see, we can dynamically change how we want to view our data with just a few clicks. When you're happy with your summary, you can then apply formatting to the appropriate columns. For example, you could format **Sum of Total Cost** as **Currency** before any formal presentation of the data.

The good thing about PivotTables is that you can explore different types of summaries with the pivot table without changing the source data. If you make a mistake that you can't figure out how to undo, you can simply delete the PivotTable worksheet and recreate the PivotTable in a new worksheet.

8.7 Filter and Sort a PivotTable

On some occasions, you may want to limit what is displayed in the PivotTable. You can sort and filter a PivotTable just like you can do to a range of data or an Excel table.

To filter a PivotTable:

1.   Click on the AutoFilter (down arrow) on the Row Labels cell.

     The pop-up menu provides a list of the row headings in your PivotTable. You can select/deselect items on this list to limit the data being displayed in the PivotTable.

2.   Uncheck **Select All.**

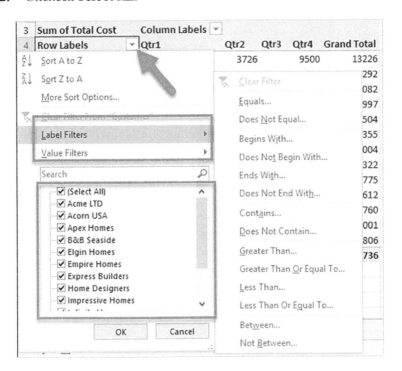

3.   Scroll through the list and manually select the items you want to display.

4.   Click **OK**.

The PivotTable will now show only the selected columns.

Applying a Custom Filter

You can also use the **Label Filters** and **Value Filters** menu commands to apply a custom filter to your PivotTable. This is done in the same way as you would do for a range or table. How to apply a custom filter to a data list in Excel is covered in detail in my Excel 2019 Basics book.

Sorting PivotTable Data

To arrange the order of your data in a PivotTable, you use the same sorting methods you would use for a range or table.

- Click on the **AutoFilter** button on the column named **Row Labels**.

- Click on **Sort A to Z** (to sort in ascending order) or **Sort Z to A** (to sort in descending order). If your column headings are dates, then you'll get **Sort Oldest to Newest** (for ascending) and **Sort Newest to Oldest** (for descending).

8.8 Present Data with PivotCharts

Another way you can present your pivot data is by using charts. In my *Excel 2019 Basics* book, I covered creating, editing, and formatting regular Excel charts. Here we will be focusing on generating charts from pivot tables. A pivot chart is simply a chart based on a pivot table. So, instead of manually aggregating your data first before creating a regular Excel chart, you can simply generate a quick pivot table and pivot chart based on the pivot table. This makes the process much faster.

To create a pivot chart based on a pivot table, follow these steps:

1. Place the cell pointer anywhere in the pivot table. On the **Insert** tab, in the **Charts** group, click on the **PivotChart** command button.

   Note that you can also find the **PivotChart** command button in the **Tools** group of the **PivotTable Analyze** tab (which is displayed on the Ribbon when the cell pointer is in the PivotTable).

2. Excel opens the **Insert Chart** dialog box which allows you to select the type and subtype of the pivot chart you want to create.

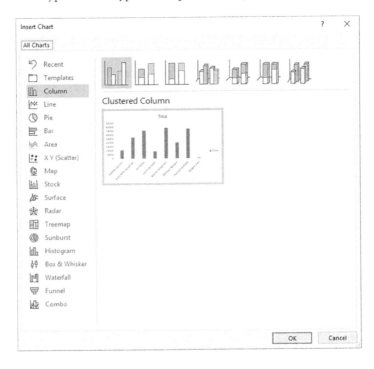

3. Select the type and subtype of the chart you want in the Insert Chart dialog box and click **OK**.

When you click OK, Excel inserts an embedded pivot chart in the worksheet with the pivot table used as the data source.

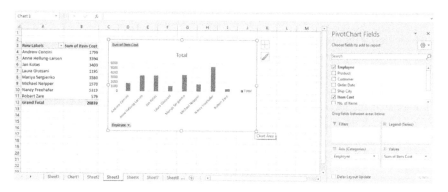

Tip: To move the chart around the screen, move your mouse pointer over the chart (the mouse pointer will change to a crosshair), then click and drag the chart to any part of the screen you want.

When you click on the PivotChart, three additional tabs appear on the Ribbon, **PivotChart Analyze**, **Design**, and **Format**. You can use commands on these tabs to redesign, modify, and format your pivot chart.

Filtering a PivotChart

After you generate a new pivot chart, you'll notice Field Buttons on the chart. These are drop-down list buttons for each of the fields represented on the chart. You can use these dropdown buttons in the pivot chart itself to filter what is represented on the chart in the same way you can do with the pivot table.

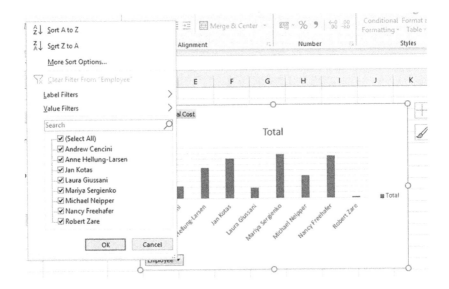

For our example above, we have the *Employee* drop-down button on the chart as that is the value being represented in the chart area.

To filter the chart, for example, if you want to exclude some names, you can click on the Employee drop-down button and uncheck **Select All**. Then you can individually select the names you want to represent in the filtered pivot chart.

To hide the Field Buttons on the chart, for example, if you want to print the chart without the buttons, do the following:

1.   On the Ribbon, click the **PivotChart Analyze** contextual tab.

2.   In the **Show/Hide** group, click **Field Buttons** (click the button's image rather than it's dropdown arrow). You can toggle this button to show or hide the field buttons on the chart.

Moving the PivotChart

To move the chart to another worksheet, do the following:

1.   Click on the pivot chart and then click on the **PivotChart Analyze** tab.

2. In the **Actions** group, click the **Move Chart** command button. Excel displays the **Move Chart** dialog box.

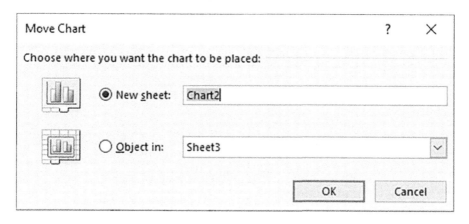

3. Select **New sheet** and in the corresponding text box, you can accept the default name provided for the new worksheet or type in another name of your choosing.

4. Click **OK** when done.

The pivot chart will be moved to a new worksheet.

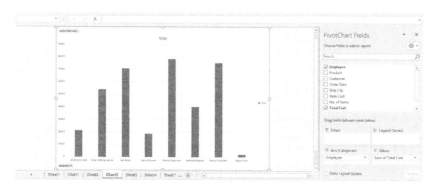

Generate a PivotTable and a PivotChart Simultaneously

You can generate a pivot table and a pivot chart simultaneously from your data list without having to generate the pivot table first.

To generate the pivot table and pivot chart together, do the following:

1. Click anywhere in the data list.
2. On the **Insert** tab click the drop-down arrow for the **PivotChart** command button.
3. Select **PivotChart & PivotTable** from the drop-down menu on the command button.
4. On the **Create PivotTable** dialog box, click the **OK** button.

Excel will create a new worksheet with the placeholders for a pivot table and a pivot chart. In the **PivotChart Fields** pane on the right side of the window, you can select the fields to go in your pivot chart, just as described in the section on manually creating a PivotTable in this chapter. As you select the fields you want for the chart in the PivotChart Fields pane, the pivot table and pivot chart will be created together.

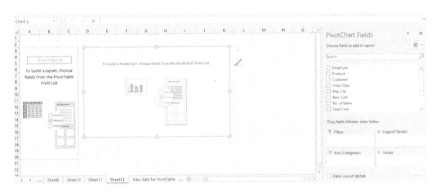

Formatting a Pivot Chart

Formatting a pivot chart is similar to formatting a regular Excel chart, which I covered in my *Excel 2019 Basics* book. If you want to learn how to edit and format charts, I recommend looking up the chapter, *Creating Charts* in my *Excel 2019 Basics* book.

9. PROTECT WORKBOOKS, WORKSHEETS, AND RANGES

E xcel provides several methods at different levels that you can use to protect your workbooks and worksheets from unauthorised access, changes to the data, moving/deleting worksheets, or renaming worksheets in your workbook.

In this chapter, we will cover how to:
- Password-protect your Excel file.
- Set different access levels for your workbook with passwords.
- Protect your workbook structure from unauthorised changes.
- Protect individual worksheets within a workbook.
- Protect specific ranges within a worksheet.

Important! Before you protect your workbook with a password, ensure that you've got the password written down and stored in a safe place where it can be retrieved if necessary. Microsoft does not provide any methods to access a password-protected Excel file where the password has been lost. Without an advanced password cracking tool, it is impossible to gain access to an Excel file that has been password-protected, if the password has been forgotten.

9.1 Password-Protect Your Workbook

To quickly encrypt your workbook with a password on your Excel workbook:

1. Click **File** > **Info** > **Protect Document** > **Encrypt with Password**.

2. At the prompt enter your password, then confirm it.

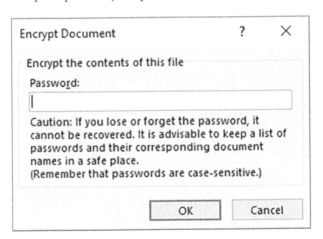

3. Click on **OK** after confirming the password.

4. Save and close the workbook.

5. When you reopen the workbook, it will prompt you for the password.

Removing the Password

On some occasions, you may want to remove a password from an Excel file. The process of setting a password encrypts the file, so you'll need to remove the encryption to remove the password.

To remove the password of an Excel file, follow the steps below:

1. Open the workbook and enter the password in the Password box.

2. Click **File** > **Info** > **Protect Workbook** > **Encrypt with Password**.

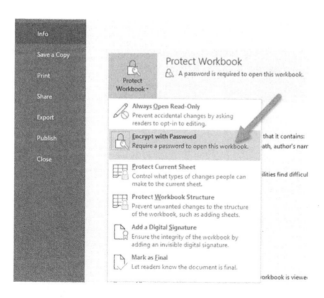

3. In the **Encrypt Document** dialog box, delete the contents of the **Password** text box.

4. Click **OK**.

5. Close and reopen the workbook. It will no longer challenge you for a password.

9.2 Set Different Access Levels

The password protection method described above enables you to quickly protect your Excel workbook from unauthorised access with a password. However, it does not provide a way to set different access levels, for example, **read-only** access and **read-write** access. To set different access levels with passwords, you need to use the older method where you save the file with a different name and insert the passwords during the process. This method allows you to set separate passwords for opening and modifying the file.

Note: Only use this method (over the encryption method described above) if you want to create different access levels for different groups of users.

To set different passwords for opening and modifying an Excel file, do the following:

1. Click on **File** > **Save As** (or **Save a Copy** if your file is on OneDrive and AutoSave is set to **On**).

2. Click on the **More options** link (which is directly under the file type field). This will open the **Save As** dialog box.

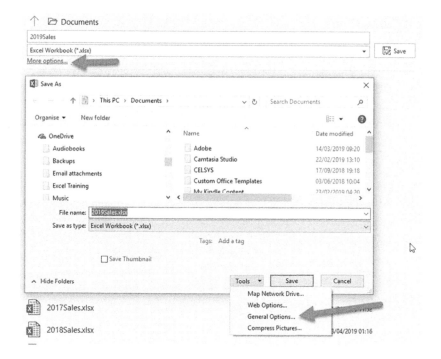

3. On the **Save As** dialog box, click on the **Tools** button and select **General Options** from the menu.

This will display the **General Options** dialog box which enables you to set one password for opening the workbook and another for modifying the workbook.

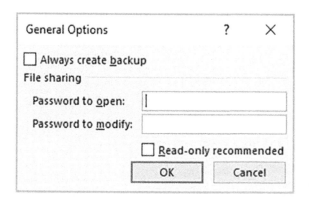

4. Enter different passwords in the **Password to modify** and **Password to open** boxes, and then click **OK**.

5. Two **Confirm Password** prompts will be displayed. Re-enter **Password to open** and **Password to modify** to confirm them.

6. In the **Save As** dialog box, in the **File name** field, enter a new name for the workbook and click **Save**. Note that you must save the file with a new name as Excel will not allow you to save it with the current name.

7. Close and reopen the workbook. This time Excel will challenge you with a prompt for a password to open the workbook. Enter the password and click **OK**.

8. Excel will display another password prompt for write-access to the workbook. Enter the write-access password in the **Password** field and click on **OK** (this is the password set in the Password to modify field).

Anyone with the password to open the workbook but not the password to modify it can open the file in read-only mode by clicking on the **Read Only** button.

Removing the Passwords Set in General Options

There may be occasions when you want to remove file protection and make the file accessible to all users. To remove the passwords set in General Options we need to delete them from General Options and save the file again.

Do the following to remove the passwords:

1. Open the Excel file with the current passwords.

2. Click on **File** to go to the backstage view and click on **Save As** (or **Save a Copy** if your file is saved on OneDrive).

3. Click on the **More options** link (which is directly under the file type text box). This will open the **Save As** window.

4. In the **Save As** dialog box, click on the **Tools** button and select **General Options** from the menu. This will display the **General Options** dialog box where you entered the passwords.

5. Delete the passwords from the **Password to modify** and **Password to open** fields and click on **OK** to dismiss the dialog box.

6. In the **Save As** dialog box, click on **Save** to save the file.

7. Close the workbook and reopen it. It will no longer prompt you for a password.

9.3 Protect the Workbook Structure

You can protect your workbook structure with a password to prevent other users from adding, moving, deleting, renaming, hiding, or viewing hidden worksheets. Note that, protecting the workbook structure is different from protecting an Excel file or worksheet with a password. When you protect your workbook structure, the file is still accessible to everyone with access to it, but they can't change the structure of the workbook.

To protect your workbook, carry out the following steps:

1. On the **Review** tab of the ribbon, in the **Protect** group, click **Protect Workbook**.

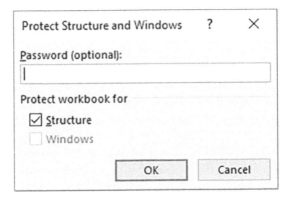

2. In the **Protect Structure and Windows** dialog box enter a password in the **Password** field.

3. Click **OK**.

4. In the **Confirm Password** dialog box, re-enter the password and click **OK**.

With the workbook protected, all the commands that involve changing the structure of the workbook, for example, add, delete, move, or rename worksheets will be disabled. To re-enable these commands, you'll need to remove the password protection.

Unprotect the Workbook Structure

To unprotect your workbook's structure, do the following:

1. On the **Review** tab of the ribbon, in the **Protect** group, click **Protect Workbook**.

2. In the **Unprotect Workbook** dialog box, enter the workbook's password and click **OK**.

9.4 Protect Worksheets

Instead of protecting the whole workbook with a password, you can protect individual worksheets and even narrow it down to restricting certain actions within the sheet. For example, you can lock certain cells in the worksheet with formulas from being editable so that other users cannot accidentally delete formulas.

In a shared workbook, users could inadvertently delete formulas as they may not be aware that some cells are calculated values rather than ordinary values. To prevent this from happening, cells with formulas are often protected in shared worksheets.

Another reason to protect parts of your worksheet is that you may have some core data that you don't want users to change. You can protect those ranges only on the worksheet.

Worksheet protection involves two steps:

1. First, unlock the cells that you want to keep editable. If you don't take this step all cells in the worksheet will be locked when you protect it.

2. Protect the worksheet with or without a password.

Step 1 - Unlock any cells/ranges that need to be editable:

1. Click on the worksheet name tab that you want to protect to select it. In the worksheet area, select the range(s) that you don't want protected.

   Tip: You can select multiple ranges by holding down the **Ctrl** key while selecting additional ranges.

2. On the **Home** tab, in the **Cells** group, click on **Format > Format Cells**.

3. Click on the **Protection** tab and clear the **Locked** checkbox.

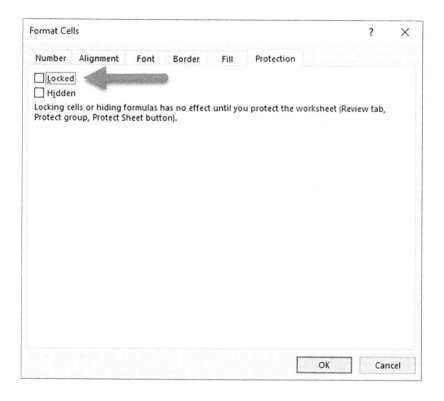

Step 2 - Protect the worksheet:

Next, you can choose specific actions that users are allowed to carry out in the worksheet.

1.   On the **Review** tab, in the **Protect** group, click **Protect Sheet**.

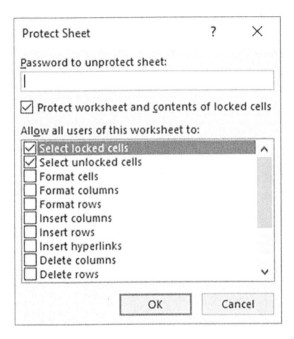

2. Ensure **Protect worksheet and contents of locked cells** is selected. This should be selected by default.

3. In the section named **Allow all users of this worksheet to**, check the actions you want users to be able to carry out on the worksheet. For example, you could allow users to insert rows and columns, sort data, format cells, use AutoFilter etc. among the many options on the list.

4. Optional: You can specify a password to lock your worksheet, but this is optional. You can protect the sheet without a password, but a user can click the **Unprotect Sheet** button to deactivate the sheet protection. If you want to prevent people from doing this, you can enter a password in the **Password to unprotect sheet** field and click **OK**. Re-enter the password at the **Confirm Password** prompt and click **OK** to complete the action.

Important! If you set a password to protect your worksheet, you'll need the password whenever you want to unprotect it. Hence, it is critical that you remember your password. Ideally, you want to have it written down somewhere under lock and key for easy retrieval if needed. If the password is lost, there are no tools provided by Microsoft to retrieve it.

Unprotect a Worksheet

In a protected worksheet, in place of the **Protect Sheet** command button on the **Review** tab, you'll see an **Unprotect Sheet** command button.

To unprotect the sheet, click the **Unprotect Sheet** command button. If it was protected with a password, you'll get a password prompt. Enter the password, and then click **OK** to unprotect the worksheet.

9.5 Protect Specific Ranges

When you protect a worksheet, by default Excel locks all cells, unless you specifically unlock some cells before you enable protection (as described above). If all cells are locked, then to access the locked parts of the sheet you have to remove the sheet protection altogether.

What if we have occasions where we want to enable some users to have access to locked ranges without removing the sheet protection?

Excel provides a solution with the **Allow Edit Ranges** command. You can password protect specific ranges in the worksheet rather than the whole sheet.

Also, if you're using a Microsoft Windows machine that is on a network domain, you can give specific users in your domain permission to edit ranges in a protected worksheet.

The process involves two steps:

1. Specify the ranges to be password protected.
2. Protect the worksheet.

Step 1 - Follow these steps to specify the ranges to be password protected:

1. If the worksheet is already protected, you need to unprotect the sheet first.

2. Select the worksheet that you want to protect by clicking on the sheet tab at the bottom of the screen.

3. On the **Review** tab, in the **Protect** group, click **Allow Edit Ranges**. Note that this command button is only available when the worksheet is unprotected.

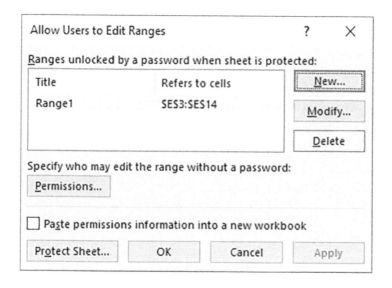

4. To add a new range that you want to be editable using a password, click **New**.

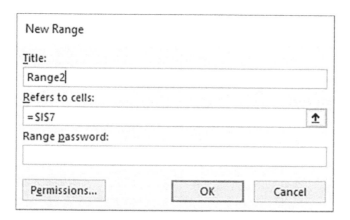

5. On the **New Range** dialog box, in the **Title** field, type the name for the range that you want to unlock.

6. In the **Refers to** cells field, you can type in the cell reference of the range, starting with an equal sign (=). Alternatively, you can click on the Collapse Dialog button (the up arrow on the field) and select the range on the worksheet. Click the Collapse Dialog button again to return to the New Range dialog box.

7. In the **Range password** field, enter a password that allows access to the range.

   Note: To use domain permissions, click the **Permissions** button and follow the process to add a domain user. This only applies to network domains with multiple user accounts.

8. Click **OK** to return to the **Allow Users to Edit Ranges** dialog box.

Step 2 - Protect the worksheet:

1. In the **Allow Users to Edit Ranges** dialog box, click the **Protect Sheet** button.

   Note: If you have closed the **Allow Users to Edit Ranges** dialog box, then click **Protect Sheet** on the **Review** tab of the Ribbon.

2. The **Protect worksheet and contents of locked cells** check box should be selected by default. If it is not you should select it.

3. In the **Allow all users of this worksheet to** list, select the actions you want users to be able to carry out on the worksheet. For example, you could allow users to insert rows and columns, sort data, format cells, or use AutoFilter, among the many options on the list.

4. In the **Password to unprotect sheet** field, enter a password and click **OK**. Re-enter the password to confirm it and click **OK** again.

   As mentioned previously, the password is optional. If you don't set a password, any user can click the **Unprotect Sheet** button on the Ribbon to unprotect the sheet.

Once a range has been protected, the user will be prompted to enter a password when they try to edit it. They'll only need to enter the password once per session.

Important! This has been mentioned earlier in this chapter but is worth repeating. If you set a password to protect your worksheet, you'll need the password whenever you want to unprotect it. Hence, it is critical that you remember your password. Ideally, you want to have it written down somewhere under lock and key for easy retrieval if needed. If you forget the password, there are no tools provided by Microsoft to retrieve it.

AFTERWORD: NEXT STEPS

Thank you for buying this book. I hope it will serve as a great Excel resource for you. The scope of this book has been kept to a selection of topics deemed more relevant to common tasks you would perform at home or work if you're an Excel power user.

If you have any questions, comments, or suggestions, please feel free to contact me at **info@excelbytes.com**.

More Help with Excel

For more help with Excel, see my other books in the **Other Books by Author** chapter. You can also visit Excel's official online help site at:

https://support.office.com/en-gb/excel

This is a comprehensive help centre for Excel. Although not an organised tutorial like this book, it is a useful resource when you're looking for help on a specific feature or tool in Excel. You'll also find resources like Excel templates that you can download and use as the starting basis for your worksheets.

APPENDIX: KEYBOARD SHORTCUTS (EXCEL FOR WINDOWS)

The Excel Ribbon comes with new shortcuts called Key Tips. To see Key Tips, press the **Alt** key when Excel is the active window.

The following table lists the most frequently used shortcuts in Excel 2019.

Keystroke	Action
F1	Opens Excel's Help window
Ctrl+O	Open a workbook
Ctrl+W	Close a workbook
Ctrl+C	Copy
Ctrl+V	Paste
Ctrl+X	Cut
Ctrl+Z	Undo
Ctrl+B	Bold
Ctrl+S	Save a workbook
Ctrl+F1	Displays or hides the ribbon
Delete key	Remove cell contents
Alt+H	Go to the Home tab
Alt+H, H	Choose a fill color
Alt+N	Go to Insert tab
Alt+A	Go to Data tab
Alt+P	Go to Page Layout tab

Alt+H, A, then C	Center align cell contents
Alt+W	Go to View tab
Shift+F10, or Context key	Open context menu
Alt+H, B	Add borders
Alt+H, D, then C	Delete column
Alt+M	Go to Formula tab
Ctrl+9	Hide the selected rows
Ctrl+0	Hide the selected columns

Access Keys for Ribbon Tabs

To go directly to a tab on the Excel Ribbon, press one of the following access keys.

Action	Keystroke
Open the Tell me box on the Ribbon.	Alt+Q
Open the File page i.e. the Backstage view.	Alt+F
Open the Home tab.	Alt+H
Open the Insert tab.	Alt+N
Open the Page Layout tab.	Alt+P
Open the Formulas tab.	Alt+M
Open the Data.	Alt+A
Open the Review.	Alt+R
Open the View.	Alt+W

To get a more comprehensive list of Excel for Windows Shortcut, press **F1** to open Excel Help and type in "Keyboard shortcuts" in the search bar.

GLOSSARY

Absolute reference
This is a cell reference that doesn't change when you copy a formula containing the reference to another cell. For example, $A$3 means the row and column have been set to absolute.

Add-in
A different application that can be added to extend the functionality of Excel. It could be from Microsoft or a third-party vendor.

Active cell
The cell that is currently selected and open for editing.

Alignment
The way a cell's contents are arranged within that cell. This could be left, centred or right.

Argument
The input values a function requires to carry out a calculation.

AutoCalculate
This is an Excel feature that automatically calculates and displays the summary of a selected range of figures on the status bar.

AutoComplete
This is an Excel feature that completes data entry for a range of cells based on values in other cells in the same column or row.

Backstage view
This is the screen you see when you click the File tab on the ribbon. It has a series of menu options to do with managing your workbook and configuring global settings in Excel.

Cell reference
The letter and number combination that represents the intersection of a column and row. For example, B10 means column B, row 10.

Chart
A visual representation of summarised worksheet data.

Conditional format
This is a format that applies only when certain criteria are met by the cell content.

Conditional formula
A conditional formula calculates a value from one of two expressions based on whether a third expression evaluates to true or false.

Delimiter
A character in a text file that is used to separate the values into columns.

Dependent
A cell with a formula that references other cells, so its value is dependent on other cells.

Dialog box launcher
In the lower-right corner of some groups on the Excel ribbon, you'll see a diagonal down-pointing arrow. When you click on the arrow it opens a dialog box containing several additional options for that group.

Digital certificate
A file with a unique string of characters that can be combined with an Excel workbook to create a verifiable signature.

Digital signature
A mathematical construct which combines a file and a digital certificate to verify the authorship of the file.

Excel table
This is a cell range that has been defined as a table in Excel. Excel adds certain attributes to the range to make it easier to manipulate the data as a table.

Fill handle
This is a small square on the lower-right of the cell pointer. You can drag this handle to AutoFill values for other cells.

Fill series
This is the Excel functionality that allows you to create a series of values based on a starting value and any rules or intervals included.

Formula
An expression used to calculate a value.

Formula bar
This is the area just above the worksheet grid that displays the value of the active cell. This is where you enter a formula in Excel.

Function
A function is a predefined formula in Excel that just requires input values (arguments) to calculate and return a value.

Goal Seek
An analysis tool that can be used to create projections by setting the goal and the tool calculates the input values required to meet the goals from a set number of variables.

Graph
A representation of summarised worksheet data, also known as a chart.

Live Preview
A preview of whatever task you want to perform based on your actual data. So, you get to see how your data will look if you carry out the command.

Locked cell
A locked cell cannot be modified if the worksheet is protected.

Macro
A series of instructions created from recording Excel tasks that automate Excel when replayed.

Named range
A group of cells in your worksheet given one name that can then be used as a reference.

OneDrive

This is a cloud storage service provided by Microsoft which automatically syncs your files to a remote drive, hence providing instant backups.

PivotChart

A specific kind of Excel chart related to a pivot table. A PivotChart can be dynamically reorganised to show different views of your data just like a pivot table.

PivotTable

This is an Excel summary table that allows you to dynamically summarise data from different perspectives. PivotTables are highly flexible, and you can quickly adjust them, depending on how you need to display your results.

Precedent

A cell that is used as a cell reference in a formula in another cell. Also see Dependent.

Quick Access Toolbar

This is a customisable toolbar with a set of commands independent of the tab and ribbon commands currently on display.

Relative reference

Excel cell references are relative references by default. This means, when copied across multiple cells, they change based on the relative position of columns and rows.

Ribbon

This is the top part of the Excel screen that contains the tabs and commands.

Scenario

An alternative set of data which you can use the compare the impact of changes in your data. This is useful when creating projections and forecasts.

Solver

An Excel add-in that enables you to create scenarios for more complex data models.

Sort

A sort means to reorder the data in a worksheet in ascending or descending order by one or more columns.

Tracer arrows
Graphical arrows used to indicate dependent or precedent cells.

Watch
The watch window can be used to display the contents of a cell in a separate window even when the cell is not visible on the screen.

What-If Analysis
A series of methods that can be used to determine the impact of changes on your data. This could include projections and forecasts.

Workbook
This is the Excel document itself and it can contain one or more worksheets.

Worksheet
A worksheet is like a page in an Excel workbook.

x-axis
The horizontal axis of a chart where you could have time intervals etc.

y-axis
This is the vertical axis of a chart, which usually depicts value data.

INDEX

ABOUT THE AUTHOR

Nathan George is a computer science graduate with several years' experience in the IT services industry in different roles, including Excel programming and providing end-user support to Excel power users. One of his main interests is using computers to automate tasks and increase productivity. As an author, he has written several technical and non-technical books.

OTHER BOOKS BY AUTHOR

Excel 2019 Basics

A Quick and Easy Guide to Boosting Your Productivity with Excel

Excel 2019 Basics covers all the essentials you need to quickly get up to speed in creating spreadsheets solutions for your data.

If you are new to Excel and the thought of spreadsheets makes your head spin, then this is the right book for you. This book will hold your hand through a step-by-step process in becoming skilled with Excel.

If you already have some Excel skills and you want to skill-up on more advanced topics like functions, Excel tables, charts, and pivot tables then this book is also for you. *Excel 2019 Basics* goes beyond introductory topics and covers topics like functions, Excel tables, and analyzing your data with charts.

This book will guide you from 'beginner' to 'skilled' with Excel within a few short hours.

For more, go to:

https://www.excelbytes.com/excel-books

Excel 2019 Functions

70 Top Excel Functions Made Easy

Do you want to delve more into Excel functions and leverage their full power in your formulas?

Excel functions are predefined formulas that make it easier and faster to create solutions for your data.

Excel 2019 Functions provides a detailed walkthrough of 70 of the most useful and relevant Excel functions in various categories including logical, reference, statistical, financial, math, and text functions.

Learn how to use many advanced functions introduced in Excel 2016/2019 like the IFS function which can replace convoluted nested IF functions.

This book also comes with lots of sample files available online that you can download as Excel files. You can copy and use the formulas in your own worksheets. *Excel 2019 Functions* will be a great resource for you whether you're a beginner or experienced with Excel.

For more, go to:

https://www.excelbytes.com/excel-books

Excel 2019 Macros and VBA

An Introduction to Excel Programming

Do you often perform repetitive tasks in Excel that can be time-consuming?

You can automate pretty much any task in Excel with a macro.

If you want to automate Excel, *Excel 2019 Macros and VBA* will be a great resource for you.

We start from the very basics of Excel automation, so you do not need any prior experience of Excel programming.

You will learn how to automate Excel using recorded macros as well as Visual Basic for Applications (VBA) code. You will learn all the programming essentials to start creating your own VBA code from scratch.

Excel 2019 Macros and VBA will enable you to create solutions that will save you time and effort, create consistency in your work, and help to minimize errors in your Excel projects.

For more, go to:

https://www.excelbytes.com/excel-books

Printed in Great Britain
by Amazon